The Art of Influencing Anyone

Make People Do Whatever You Want

Niall Cassidy

Copyright © 2008, 2013 by Niall Cassidy

Reprinted 2014

All rights reserved. No part of this publication may be reproduced, distributed, or transmitted in any form or by any means, including photocopying, recording, or other electronic or mechanical methods, without the prior written permission of the publisher, except in the case of brief quotations embodied in critical reviews and certain other non-commercial uses permitted by copyright law. For permission requests, write to the publisher, addressed "Attention: Permissions Coordinator," at the email address below.

Email: niallcassidy2013@gmail.com
Blog: niallcassidy.blogspot.com

ISBN: 978-988-12242-2-4

Table of Content

Preface   5

Part I: Introduction

Chapter 1: A Miracle at Kyle's   10

Part II: Invincible Credibility

Chapter 2: Compelling Arguments   36
Chapter 3: Prophetic Predictions   63

Part III: Impeccable Marketing

Chapter 4: Instant Attention   93
Chapter 5: Covert Advertising   125

Part IV: Immaculate Conditioning

Chapter 6: Rapid Rapport   158
Chapter 7: Burning Desires   190

Part V: Conclusion

Chapter 8: Mrs. McKinsey Bought — 224

About the Author — 249

Preface

Ever since I wrote the Art of Influencing Anyone, I have been giving out free copies of the book to friends and their friends. One day, when I was in a gathering, a stranger suddenly came to me and asked, "Are you the bloke who wrote the Art of Influencing Anyone?"

"Yes, I am." As I replied, I scrutinised the chap who spoke to me. He was a good-looking young fellow in his early twenties. I didn't think I had ever met him before though.

"It's nice to meet you. My name is John," he said. "I read your book. It was given to me by a friend. I must say I'm very impressed by your ideas."

"I'm glad to hear that," I said. As a writer, nothing delights me more than compliments from a reader.

"And I want to let you know that your book really helped me a lot. I'm now enjoying much more success at work than I used to."

It turned out that John was actually a young employee in a reputable corporation. Even though it was generally considered a privilege to work there, the office politics at his workplace were extremely complex and mind-boggling. He felt that going to work was like going to war every day.

"Even many colleagues who are older and more experienced than me had trouble as well. One of them was a very capable worker, but since he had very poor communication skills, he couldn't get along with his manager, and he eventually got fired."

"I'm sure that it must be a very unpleasant job," I said.

"That's true. However, I had no choice but to bite the bullet. I am the only breadwinner of a poor family, and I live from pay packet to pay packet. This is the job that pays me the most generous salary, and I won't be able to find another one that pays the same money if I quit."

Then the young man told me about his family. He was the only son of a wealthy family, and his father ran a respectable business. Sadly, his father made some poor decisions, and his whole business was destroyed overnight. After filing for bankruptcy, his father couldn't swallow his pride and move on, so he committed suicide.

The event completely changed their lives. His mother, who had been a rich man's wife for many years, had not accumulated much working experience, so she ended up as a humble cashier in a supermarket. As for John himself, his weekend activities changed from hanging out in clubs to working part-time in an upmarket department store.

John decided that it was not what he wanted for the rest of his life, so he became determined to climb higher in society and lead a better life. This was exactly why he didn't hesitate to read my book from cover to cover when his friend told him that my book could help him to do better in his company.

"When I finally graduated from university, I immediately got hired by the company in which I'm now working. Since it's a global conglomerate, I was quite satisfied at first, but I soon realised that, to survive in such a competitive environment, you have to calculate like a computer in the office every day. It's not just about how hard you work, but also how much you get along with others without being taken advantage of."

"So how did you deal with all the office politics?" I asked.

"This was where your book came into play. After reading it, I was suddenly aware of the tactics my colleagues used to try and manipulate me, and more importantly, I was able to handle them much more effectively than before. There are many other fresh graduates who joined the company around the same time as me, but they are not as fortunate as I am, and they frequently get into troubles."

"I'm really glad that my book helped you."

"Strangely enough, once I demonstrated that I knew how to handle their challenges, my colleagues started to treat me with more respect. And since they knew that it wasn't easy to take advantage of me, they switched their attention to seeking more innocent victims."

I smiled and agreed with him. I certainly knew what he was talking about, as I had been in a similar position before – as the victim.

After that, he sighed, "When many fresh graduates first come out to work, they have no idea that many people in the working world are actually sharks. Once they discover that you are susceptible, they will not hesitate to tear you apart piece by piece before you even realise what's going on. Now thanks to your work, I'm no longer a poor little fish who could be eaten easily in the corporate ocean."

I really liked that analogy, and I think it applies to many grown-ups in the corporate world as well. While I do not want to promote an abusive philosophy in treating your co-workers, I'm sure that many people feel bullied by their managers/customers every day. If it is your case, then perhaps it's time to contemplate what you could learn from John's story.

Niall Cassidy
4th June, 2014

1. A Miracle at Kyle's

A Miracle in a Start-up Boutique

Mr. Kyle Thomson was a retired fashion designer. In an attempt to avoid retirement boredom, he started a small retail fashion shop called Kyle's Boutique. However, since it was his first time ever doing business, he lacked the experience to manage his shop properly, and thus it had been losing money every month since its opening.

Needless to say, it was not a very encouraging result, and Mr. Thomson was extremely disappointed. However, just when he was about to give it up altogether, a miracle suddenly happened in the shop.

One day, when Mr. Thomson checked his business ledger, he was totally surprised. The sales had more than doubled in just a few weeks. In addition to that, he even found that some of the most expensive items, which had never been sold, had disappeared from the shelf as well.

Mr. Thomson was very perplexed. What had happened? Had his shop caught the attention of a very wealthy customer who liked his clothes a lot? Or had someone written a very positive recommendation in a local newspaper column? Or was it the eventual success of his indefatigable comment-writing about his shop on various websites and online forums?

Later, he found out that it was none of the above. There were no particularly rich customers who had stumbled upon his shop. No magazines or newspapers had written about it. Nor was it related to all his anonymous recommendations on the Internet. All these were caused by an accident of hiring the right person.

Super Salesgirl

Scarlett was a university student who had just started to work part-time in Mr. Thomson's boutique. She had never been employed as a full-time salesperson before, nor ever participated in any related training courses. When Mr. Thomson hired her, he thought she was just another ordinary university girl who wanted to earn some extra income while studying.

Despite that, just in the first month of work, she had already sold much more things than anyone could imagine. For every 10 transactions completed in the shop, five or six of them would be contributed by Scarlett. All the other people working in the shop were stunned by her performance, and they all saw her as a godsend for the business.

Of course, Mr. Thomson was delighted by Scarlett, but at the same time, he was also extremely curious about how she could achieve that, so he personally invited her for coffee and a chat in a nearby café. After they had settled down, Mr. Thomson told her:

"Scarlett, I am extremely grateful for your contribution to my shop. As an encouragement to keep up your good work, I will give you a bonus equal to 50 per cent of your salary this month, and I will raise your salary permanently if you can maintain your amazing feat."

"I am very grateful," said Scarlett, "It is very important for me because I am from a very poor family. It will be great if I can afford to live on my own without spending a quid from my family."

"I am glad that I can help," said Mr. Thomson. "Naturally, I am very curious how you could achieve your result. Would you mind telling me more about the secret of your success?"

"There is no secret at all," laughed Scarlett, "It is just that I am able to speak to the customers better than other people in the shop."

"And what do you mean by speaking better than others?" asked Mr. Thomson.

"It means…"

"Scarlett!"

A voice behind them interrupted their conversation.

A Horrible Customer

When Mr. Thomson looked back and tried to identify the interrupter, he was surprised to find someone whom he did not want to see.

The voice came from Mrs. McKinsey, a hideously troublesome old widow. She was a very cagey and stingy customer who always haggled whenever she wanted to buy something, and always complained about any imperfection she saw, no matter how trivial it was. It was such a pain to do business with her that there were a couple of times when Mr. Thomson was tempted to tell her not to come back to his shop again.

Despite that, Mr. Thomson had to be polite, so he greeted Mrs. McKinsey:

"Mrs. McKinsey, good afternoon! It's very fine weather, isn't it?"

"Indeed, Mr. Thomson," said Mrs. McKinsey. "And how is it going, Scarlett?"

"All going well," said Scarlett. "Did your daughter like the black blazer that you bought her last week?"

"Yes, she did!" said Mrs. McKinsey. "Thanks very much for your suggestions. She liked it a lot!"

"Hold on a minute," said Mr. Thomson. "Was it that elegant slimfit jacket in black that went last week?"

"Exactly that one," said Scarlett.

Mr. Thomson was perplexed. That jacket was one of the most expensive items in his shop, but Mrs. McKinsey only ever went after the cheapest ones. It was breaking news indeed. Had she mutated into a completely different person?

After Mrs. McKinsey went away, Mr. Thomson asked Scarlett:

"How on earth did you manage to get her to buy that blazer?"

"Well, she was actually very reluctant to buy anything at first, but having talked to her a few times before, I was able to understand what she liked most, and I started working there."

"How exactly did your conversation go?" asked Mr. Thomson. He was very eager to know.

Scarlett began to recount exactly what had happened on that day, and explained how she had got the old woman to buy the blazer. Mr. Thomson realised that the way she spoke to the customers was very different from that of the other people.

It Is Good, So Do It.

People often feel helpless when they have to persuade someone to do something. On one hand, we are all social animals who cannot avoid interaction with other people. No matter you are a salesman with a target to meet, a parent trying to teach your kids to behave, or a manager trying to improve your team's performance, you always want others to listen to you. It makes your life easier.

However, many of us do not find it easy to get people to listen to us. It is not all that unusual for your customers to reject you, your kids to disobey you, or people at work to ignore your ideas. At the same time, perhaps you find it impossible to understand how a particular person can manage to become a top salesman, have kids who always behave, and get the attention of everyone in the office whenever he has an idea.

So why can some people become better persuaders than most others? It certainly does not depend on their having a higher level of intelligence than the rest of us –

in fact, it is more often the more "intelligent" people who have trouble communicating with others, because they may be prone to believing that others are too stupid to understand them. Instead, what stands between the good and bad persuaders is often the right methods and techniques.

When most people try to persuade others, they often follow a monotonic formula which is known as: "It Is Good, So Do It." For example, when an insurance agent tries to persuade someone to buy a life insurance policy from him, he usually says something like this:

"Insurance is not only a protection for yourself, but also for your loved ones. I once had a client who bought an insurance policy from me fifteen years ago. His family consisted of a full-time housewife and three little children. Five years ago, he was killed in an accident. If he had not bought insurance, then not only would his wife have been forced to work again, but his children could also have been forced out of school. Luckily, with the indemnity they were able to continue to live comfortably."

Basically, the agent is giving evidence that buying insurance is useful, and his prospect is able to understand the logic of what he is trying to illustrate. However, to the prospect, it is just like watching a tragic film in a cinema. He will probably think, "I can't argue against you, but I have been without any life insurance for many years, and I am still fine. In addition, I know that you are telling me this just because you want to sell me insurance, so I will take it with a pinch of salt."

Even if you are not a salesman, you might encounter a similar situation. For example, when a father wants his son to study hard, he can tell him:

"Son, it is important to work hard and get good grades. According to a latest survey by the BBC, those who do not have a degree are paid at a level close to the minimum wage. It means that you are going to end up with a nasty job like your dad if you don't work hard."

In the above example, the father points out the horrible consequences of not studying hard, supported by the latest statistics – but do you think the son will listen to him and start to work hard immediately?

Very unlikely that he will, because even though what the father says is correct, the son will still find excuses not to study. At first, he may in some way appreciate that his father is right. However, after two or three times, he will find his father very annoying, and start to rationalise to himself: "There are many successful people in the world, like Steve Jobs and Bill Gates, who never got a university degree. Having a degree does not mean everything." Later, he may even think: "Being rich does not mean everything. It is more important to live happily when I am alive."

In other words, we all like to convince others by using logic, but logic alone is hardly enough to change people. If it were, then there would not be millions of people smoking every day, despite the proven hazards of such a habit; or anyone risking his whole fortune on the gambling table, despite the overwhelming odds against his winning. Therefore, logical reasons should never be the first things to pursue when trying to persuade someone. So, what should you do instead to persuade people?

Character over Content

In communication, there is a saying that what you say is not as important as how you say it. While this is certainly true, it is worth pointing out that how you say it is still not as important as who says it. No matter who you are speaking to, people often place more emphasis on the identity of the speaker than the content of his speech.

Here is a simple example. A doodle from a child is regarded as a piece of cheap rubbish, but a similar work from Picasso is considered a work of art, which carries an astronomical price. To the untrained eye, the two do not look very different, but if people know that it is painted by a famous artist, then their perception will change immediately, and they will think: "Oh, if it is from Picasso, it must be good. If I fail to understand it, it must be my problem."

To further illustrate this point, let us revisit a famous hoax in academia. For those who are not familiar with this world, researchers often publish their essays and reports in academic journals in order to exchange findings and ideas. However, since there are so many researchers from different universities and institutions, a journal cannot possibly publish every submission received. So how do the editors choose?

In principle, the editors select the most innovative and insightful papers, but the number of submissions is so overwhelming that they simply do not have time to go through every one. So they use a simpler method: they first look at those by the more famous and renowned researchers – on the basis that if an author is well regarded in the field, then his papers are unlikely to be too bad.

This is where the aforementioned hoax comes in. In 1996, Professor Alan Sokal of New York University submitted an article to an academic journal, *Social Text*. The article was of very poor quality, and, as the author put it, consisted of "fawning references, grandiose quotations, and outright nonsense", and was "structured around the silliest quotations he could find about mathematics and physics."

Nevertheless, Sokal's article was accepted and published, proving that even an "intellectually rigorous" academic journal could be fooled into printing an article "liberally salted with nonsense" if written by someone who worked in a university, and had a PhD.

Later, this result was replicated in a more formal experiment by sociologist Robb Willer. University students were randomly separated into two groups to study Sokal's hoax article. The first group was informed that the author was a famous expert, while the second group was told that the article had been written by a student. Consistent with the earlier story, the result was that the "expert" group made more positive comments about the article than the "student" group.

All the above results demonstrate that the identity of the speaker is more important than what he actually says. If you do not have the respect and trust of your audience, then no matter how brilliant your speech is, they will still refuse to believe you. On the other hand, if you can establish authority in the eyes of your audience, then no matter how mediocre your speech is, people will still listen to you. By the way, never underestimate the power of authority, because – as you will see in the following experiment – an authority figure is capable of influencing people to an extent that you could never imagine.

Obedience to Authority

The American psychologist Stanley Milgram once conducted a famous experiment, which demonstrated that people would obey the instructions of authority figures even when the instructions conflicted with their consciences.

The setup of the experiment involved a task in which, under the instruction of the experimenter, a volunteer had to train a student to perform a memory task. Each time the student failed, the volunteer would deliver an electric shock to him by pressing a button. Each time the electric shock was administered, the student expressed discomfort in front of the volunteer. To make it worse, the voltage of the electric shock increased after each delivery.

At first, the volunteer seemed reluctant to deliver the punishment, but each time he refused, the experimenter simply said one of the following:

- "Please continue."

- "The experiment requires that you continue."

- "It is absolutely essential that you continue."

- "You have no other choice, you must go on."

In the original version of the experiment, more than 60 per cent of the volunteers obeyed the experimenter through to the end, and delivered the final 450-volt electric shock, despite their seeing how the student suffered in front of their eyes.

Of course, there were no real electric shocks, and the "student" was, in fact, an actor, so that there was no actual harm to anyone in the experiment. Nevertheless, it shows that most people are very likely to yield to an authority figure, even if what he recommends does not seem right to them. To explain this paradoxical phenomenon, let us consider a kind of insect that we often see – moths.

It is a well-known phenomenon that moths fly into fire at night, and end up killing themselves. Why are those insects so stupid? Can they not feel the heat? The answer is that moths do it because it is a misfiring of their primitive instinct. They have an innate disposition to be attracted to light, because they use a bright light source such as the moon for navigation. However, since they are unable to distinguish between celestial bodies and fire, they sometimes follow the wrong guide, and it leads to their untimely demise.

It is similar with human beings. We have an innate disposition to obey figures of authority. When we are young, we rely on our parents and teachers to make decisions for us. When we grow up, we seek advice from professionals such as lawyers, doctors and university professors, because they are supposed to know more than we do in their own professions, and they are able to teach us what to do when we need their professional knowledge.

In fact, people usually believe that if an expert tells them that something is right, it probably will be, even though it may not seem so. For instance, in the experiment above, the volunteers followed the instructions of the experimenter to deliver electric shocks to the "student", despite the fact that he looked very uncomfortable. They probably thought: "Well, the professor is experienced and knows more than I do. I am certain that he would not do something that runs counter to the proper conduct of a researcher. Since I am paid to do this anyway, I'd better just follow what he says."

All these examples demonstrate that people often follow the words of authorities with total faith. Therefore, the first thing that you need to do when you are aiming to persuade others is not to tell people how good your ideas are, but to convince them that you are an expert to whom they should listen. Unfortunately, in most cases, it is not an easy thing to do. Is there any way to make other people trust you in a very short time?

Give Me the Evidence

No one would trust a stranger without a reason, and therefore, in order to make people believe in you, you must show them something that will make you sound more reliable. To demonstrate your credibility, there are two kinds of proof that you can show them: "external" and "internal" ones.

"External" proofs refer to any objective qualification or brand name that is widely recognised. For example, if you are a professor of physics at the University of Cambridge, then you can very easily make people believe you when you talk about physics, because Cambridge University is one of the most famous research centres in the world, and it requires the highest qualifications to teach there. In other words, your affiliation is a yardstick of your credibility.

Do not be disappointed if you do not work for a famous company. For others, your credibility can be based on your track record. Everyone knows that J. K. Rowling made a fortune by writing the Harry Potter series. If she wants to publish a new book now, many publishers will fight to do it, because they have seen her success in the Harry Potter series, and are confident that her new book will sell very well. It is worth mentioning that, way back, before she published her first book, it was a completely different story.

When Rowling completed the first book of the Harry Potter series, the manuscript was sent to a large number of publishers, and was rejected by 12 of them, including big names such as Penguin and HarperCollins.

It was eventually taken up by a small London publisher called Bloomsbury, of which the chairman accepted it only because his daughter happened to read it and liked it. Once again, this shows that people are often more concerned about who you are than what you actually have to offer.

Therefore, if you do possess an impressive background or history, do not hesitate to let others know. If you are the author of a best-selling book, it will help you to get a better offer from publishers. If you are a fresh graduate who has a first class distinction from a top university, it will help you to find a job in a prestigious firm. If you are a man who has a juicy job with a lovely salary, it will be easier for you to chase a girl you fancy.

Unfortunately, if you do not come from a great institution, or do not have a great track record, what can you do? In this case, you may have to pretend to be bigger than you actually are in order to inspire confidence. Suppose you have just started your own company and you want to find customers, but because you are new, no one is confident enough to do business with you. How can you tackle this problem?

One of the tricks that you can use is called "expectation management". To put it plainly, it means to mislead others without lying. In order to understand how it works, let us consider the following story.

The Million-Pound Cheque

Mr. Rye was a young entrepreneur. During the Internet Boom in the late Nineties, he made the bold move of investing all his savings in the stock market, and multiplied his wealth more than tenfold. After the bull market was over, he used the money to buy a small factory, and began his career as a businessman.

Unfortunately, since he was so new, no one was confident enough to do business with him. No suppliers wanted to give him raw materials, no customers believed that he could deliver on time, and no bankers had the confidence to loan him any money. As a result, even after he had tried many different methods to open opportunities, Mr. Rye was still unable to do business with anyone.

Mr. Rye realised that he could not go on like that. In order to survive, he must do something special to effect a change. He somehow had to give people the confidence to do the first deal with him, and if that was successful, everything would follow. However, just how could he convince anyone enough to enable him to make the first move? After countless sleepless nights, he finally came up with an idea.

Fortunately, Mr. Rye's father was a well-connected businessman, and using his network, Mr. Rye Jr. managed to make an appointment with Mr. John Bolton, one of the leading businessmen in the younger man's industry. When they met, Mr. Rye told Mr. Bolton:

"Mr. Bolton, you are a very experienced businessman, and I am sure you know that I am here because I need some help from you. However, what I would like to ask from you is completely reasonable, and it will not cost a quid from you."

"So what do you want? Do you want me to introduce clients to you, or do you want someone to loan you money?" asked Mr. Bolton.

"No, that's not the case at all. All I want from you is a cheque," said Mr. Rye.

"You want a cheque from me?"

"Yes, a cheque for the sum of one million pounds, which must be signed by you. However, I promise I will never cash it," said Mr. Rye.

"What do you want to do with it?" asked Mr. Bolton.

Mr. Rye started to explain exactly what he was planning to do. After the explanation, Mr. Bolton was impressed by the young man in front of him, and promised to give him the cheque.

After that, whenever Mr. Rye met potential clients, he always took out the cheque and told them:

"I won't blame you if you do not believe me, because I am quite new. However, you have to believe in the people who are supporting me. Look at this cheque! Do you see who is ordering from me? It's Mr. John Bolton! The leader in your industry! Do you know why Mr. Bolton has confidence in me? Because my father is a very good friend of his, and he is one of the biggest supporters of my business!"

And since Mr. Bolton was so famous, many bankers, suppliers and customers were convinced by the cheque to give Mr. Rye the money, materials and orders to enable him to make the first move of his business. Soon after that, Mr. Rye's enterprise grew very fast, and he became one of the richest people in the country.

Proving without Proof

In the above story, Mr. Rye used the cheque to create a false impression of his business strength, and made people believe that he had some very powerful people behind him. To put it in another way, he borrowed the credibility of another person and used it for himself. Unfortunately, while this is certainly a powerful idea, it is not readily applicable to everyone in an everyday situation, because most people do not have that kind of network to get an influential figure to help them.

What happens if you have no good "external" proofs, and are unable to borrow any from other people? In that case, you will need to provide "internal" proof to support yourself. Internal proofs refer to intangible qualities such as professional knowledge and clarity of communication. Here is a little example to demonstrate the point.

Imagine that you visit two nutrition experts for dietary advice. The first expert is very famous, frequently appears on television and has written a lot of books. However, when you ask him for advice, he gives you no more than the common sense that even a child could tell you. The second expert is not at all well-known, but when you talk to him you find that his suggestions offer something that you have never realised before, and you feel that you could learn a lot from him. Which expert do you choose?

Most of us would prefer the second one, because while the first expert looks credible, the second is able to show a greater genuine credibility by giving you some really valuable advice. By demonstrating adequate knowledge and expertise, you can leave a good impression on your customers, so that next time they will immediately remember you when they need anything related to your profession.

However, you are probably wondering: "But if I do not have very much professional knowledge, how can I still talk like an expert to impress others?" The good news is: you do not really need to be a real expert, because as long as you look convincing, people will still believe in you.

In the field of education studies, there is a well-known experiment called the Dr. Fox Lecture. For this, an actor, pretending to be a professor, gave a lecture on education theories. He was coached and instructed to deliver a talk, which was filled with "an excessive use of double talk, neologisms, non sequiturs, and contradictory statements". The actor then gave the same lecture to three different groups of real experts which, in total, consisted of 55 psychiatrists, psychologists, educators, graduate students and other professionals. Would anyone in the audience be able to smell something wrong and uncover the whole prank?

The answer was no! On the contrary, they all made overwhelmingly positive comments about Dr. Fox. How on earth could all these supposedly knowledgeable people be fooled by an actor, who in reality had absolutely no idea what he was talking about? The answer is surprisingly simple: in any kind of communication, it is not about how good you actually are, but how good you appear to be.

During the training before the "lecture", the actor was instructed to adopt a lively demeanour, convey warmth towards his audience, and intersperse his nonsensical comments with humorous anecdotes. The audience, despite being professionals, were effectively "seduced" by his charisma, and enjoyed the lecture. In other words, the so-called lecturer's talk style had completely masked a "meaningless, jargon-filled, and confusing presentation".

If even professionals can be fooled in such a way, how much easier would it be to mesmerise the customers you see every day? However, even though it is really not that difficult to do, you will still need to know the right methods to achieve it. In the following two chapters, you will learn two very important skills, which have the potential to make people worship you in a very short time.

2. Compelling Arguments

The Murder of Roger Acworth

Sir Roger Acworth was a millionaire in the United Kingdom. Although he was very famous, he had a personality so unpleasant that he had more enemies than friends. It was rumoured that he had had serious conflicts with his business partners, involving millions of pounds, which had generated hatred between them.

So it was not altogether surprising that he was found dead at two o'clock one morning when he was thought to be working alone in his study. A maid in the house reported that someone had visited Sir Roger without an appointment earlier in the night, and she had heard them arguing in the study at the estimated time of death.

Now, here are two statements that describe the possible scenario on the night of Sir Roger's death:

• An unknown visitor killed Sir Roger in the study on the night of the murder.

- An unknown visitor killed Sir Roger in the study on the night of the murder, after an argument which could not be reconciled.

Which one do you think is the most likely description of what happened that night? Before you continue reading, pause for a moment and think.

The above passage is actually modified from a famous experiment by American psychologists Amos Tversky and Daniel Kahneman. When it was first conducted, most people ranked the second statement more likely than the first one – i.e. "Someone killed him after an argument" was seen as more likely than: "Someone killed him".

Most people will think the same that the second statement is more likely, because it fits the description better. However, this is logically improbable. If you also chose the second statement, then think about this simpler example:

- Tom is a European.

- Tom is a German.

Which one do you think is more likely to be true? Of course the first one is more likely, because while a German is by definition a European, not every European is a German.

This is also true for the above murder problem: whereas the first statement only stated that someone killed Sir Roger, the second had an additional requirement that they had an argument before the murder. In other words, in order for the second statement to be true, the first one has also to be true. So how is it that the second statement is more likely to be true than the first one? (Note: in the story it was never said that the visitor actually killed Sir Roger.)

This little experiment illustrates an illogical habit in human thinking: even though the first statement is more logically probable, we are more inclined to believe in the second. The reason is that the second statement gives us more information about the big picture, and the human mind thinks that whatever gives us the big picture is more likely to give us the truth.

Particularity Implies Truth

Let us consider another example. Suppose that the police caught two suspects for the murder of Sir Roger, and interrogated them to find out their whereabouts on the night in question. The first suspect said:

"I was drinking with my friends in a pub in central London. We were watching a football match between Chelsea and Liverpool. I was eating as we watched the match. The final score was a one-one draw. After the match I took the Underground and went home straight away."

The second suspect told the police:

"I was drinking with three friends in a pub in central London. We were watching a football match between Chelsea and Liverpool on a surprisingly big, hundred-inch screen. I was having fish and chips with a pint of Carlsberg as we watched the match. The final score was a one-one draw after a late leveller from Chelsea. After the match I hopped on the Central line at about eleven and went home straight away."

Which story do you find more "real"? Even though both stories are virtually identical, the second one sounds more believable to most people because it is able to provide more particulars about the experience of the teller. In fact, when you are trying to determine whether or not a person is telling you the truth, one of the most convenient ways to test him is to ask him to provide more particulars.

When we tell lies and make things up, it is usually very hard to give the particulars correctly, and there are two reasons for this. Firstly, providing more particulars gives people more opportunities to prove your testimony to be false. For instance, in the above story, the second suspect claimed that he watched the football match in the pub, which had a hundred-inch screen. If the police were to visit the pub later and find that there was no such screen, they could immediately prove that he was lying.

Secondly, coming up with particulars requires thinking. If something does not exist in your memory, you cannot come up with it out of the blue very quickly. It requires research to "proofread" your story so that every detail is consistent with the truth. Suppose the second suspect was Sir Roger's killer, and his story about watching football in a pub was a lie. In order to tell this lie, he would have had to visit the pub beforehand to observe its details. He would have had to see how large the screen was, and the sort of food that was on the menu. In other words, the more detailed your lie is, the more homework it takes to make it look true.

Therefore, if a person is lying, he will usually prefer not to give too many details. In other words, the number of details that you give is a very good indicator of your believability. So when you are telling the truth, you should come up with as many details as possible, in order to sound more convincing to your listeners.

Stand out in a Job Interview

One of the most common situations in which to apply this idea is when you attend a job interview. Usually, one of the first things to be discussed is a candidate's qualifications. For example, if a fresh graduate with no working experience is interviewing for a trainee position in a bank, he may say something like this:

"During last summer, I worked in the Union Bank of Switzerland as an intern. My primary duty was to draft public relations materials including news releases, fact sheets, status reports and so on. I was also responsible for updating and maintaining a series of databases. I learned a lot about the internal operation of an investment bank during that time."

This is a common answer that you will often hear in a job interview. Surely, it is a very clear introduction which points out the most important experience of the candidate – internship in a famous investment bank. It also outlines the exact duties of the candidate during the internship, so that the interviewer can understand exactly what he has done. Normally, with such a great internship experience, the candidate will stand a reasonable chance of being hired.

However, his answer has a small problem in that there are too few details about his experience during the intern job. If the candidate wants to look more impressive, he can change the above paragraph into something like this:

"During last summer, I worked in the Union Bank of Switzerland as an intern. My main duty was to draft public relations materials such as news releases and fact sheets. However, I had no experience of writing such things before, so I actually wrote some very laughable things in the beginning. Luckily, the people there are very nice, and they did not mind correcting me and answering my questions.

"In addition to that, I was also responsible for updating and maintaining a series of databases. Every day, I had to input different data about the clients, the marketing materials and some other administrative information. Since I am not very good at technical computer stuff, I did not begin very smoothly. So to make sure that I would be able to do my job well, I voluntarily stayed behind after work in order to learn how to manage it.

"Even though it was hard work, I felt that it was all worth it, because I learned a lot about the internal operation of an investment bank during that time."

In this new version, the candidate does not only make the experience more "real", but he is also able to show his respect for the job by staying behind to learn how to do it properly. Therefore, don't just tell people what you have done, but tell them what it is like when you do the things that you claim to have done.

Don't Tell Me, Show Me

This idea is also applicable to any other question in a job interview. Another very common one is: "Why do you consider yourself suitable for this position?" Usually people give answers such as: "I have many years of experience" – "I am very attentive to details" – "I am very hard-working", and so on. Needless to say, these are only very general descriptions, which are unlikely to impress any interviewer. You need to be more specific, and give more details to illustrate your point.

As a general rule, when you want to tell people that you have a certain quality, you should avoid saying that directly. For instance, if you want to prove that you are a hardworking person, you should never just say: "I am a very hard-working person," because the listener will immediately think: "Everyone says he works hard. Who doesn't?"

Instead, you should recount some previous experience in which you had to work hard to overcome a problem, and again you should describe the situation in detail. For example, you could tell the interviewer a story like this:

"My first job after I graduated from university was working as an assistant in a stock brokerage firm. I still remember that it was a very interesting experience, because when I went to the interview, the manager said that they needed me to be able to work immediately.

"However, the regulation required me to have a licence which I did not have. The manager told me that he would give me a month to get it, so that if I could complete and pass the licensing examination by then, he would hire me.

"That was a very hard task. The licensing exam required me to study materials equivalent to a three-hundred-page textbook, which was very difficult to memorise in just one month, and I heard that many people had to take the examination at least twice to pass, so doing it in just one month is almost impossible.

"Nevertheless, the economy was in a bad state at that time, and I was determined to get that job. I went to the public library every day, including Saturday and Sunday, and studied there for at least four hours at a time. Luckily in the end, I did pass the examination and I got the job."

When the interviewer hears the story, he will immediately get the impression that you are a really hard-working person, which is much more persuasive than simply telling him directly: "I am very hard-working." In other words, it is less effective to tell people who you are than it is to show them that you are the kind of person you claim to be.

Therefore, whenever you discuss anything with your listeners, you should always give enough details to be convincing. However, as you try to provide more facts, it is very easy to make the dangerous mistake of giving too much data, and you can end up confusing the listener. How can you give enough details without sounding confusing? In order to understand how to do that, let us go back to the story of Scarlett.

A Lesson in Ballroom Attire

It was mentioned in the last chapter that Scarlett secured a lot of new customers for Mr. Thomson. One of the customers was a university girl called Ruth, who worked as a part-time waitress in a café nearby. Scarlett had talked to her a couple of times in the café, so she recognised Ruth at once when she came into the shop.

She greeted her: "Hi there, are you looking for anything?"

"I'm looking for some new clothes for a ball," replied Ruth.

"Is it a formal one, or is it more like a dressing-up one?"

"A formal one," said Ruth. "My boyfriend is bringing me to a ball by Junior Chamber International. I've recently lost a lot of weight, so my old clothes don't fit me any more and I need to buy some new ones."

"I see. I'm sure you'll have a great time there!" said Scarlett.

"Yes! I've heard that you can meet a lot of professionals who could be helpful to your future career."

"Indeed. So I guess you would consider dressing professionally to leave an impression?"

"Dress professionally? What do you mean?"

"Let me put it this way. When you're working as a waitress, you must see a lot of people in the café every day. Have you ever had the experience that, just by seeing how a customer dresses, you could immediately guess whether he is working-class or middle-class?"

"Oh, I see what you mean."

"Therefore, it would help if you could wear a dress that can make you look like a young professional. There are two fashionable styles that are very popular among working young women these days. You might want to consider them."

"Could you tell me what they are?"

"Sure." Scarlett then showed Ruth a dress. "The first one is a bodycon dress with neck lace. It hugs your body firmly to outline your figure, but is also soft enough to be very comfortable on your skin. It is glamorous and beautiful, and you're sure to get a lot of attention."

Then Scarlett gave Ruth a second dress. "Another choice is a high-slit maxi dress. It gained a lot of attention recently when a famous actress wore it during the Cannes Film Festival. It has an elegant design with a stylish high cut, which adds a sexy element to the dress. Given its popularity, it will be a sure-fire head-turner at the ball!"

Ruth tried on the two dresses that Scarlett had shown her, and said, "Both of them look good. Which one do you think is better?"

"Well, when we consider what to wear, there are usually two factors to consider," said Scarlett.

"What are they?" asked Ruth.

"The first thing to consider is the body shape. You are tall, and one of your biggest advantages is your long, refined legs. I think you could maximise your beauty by showing more of your legs with the high-slit maxi. It will add emphasis to your slim and healthy body."

"I see. And what's the second factor?" Ruth asked.

"Secondly," Scarlett continued, "you also have to consider the situation for which you are wearing the dress. In an event with a lot of professional people, it is important to make people remember you as a cultivated and mature lady. While both dresses could no doubt achieve that, the maxi dress has two advantages. Firstly, it has a more artistic design. Secondly, as I said, it was worn by a celebrity in a film festival recently, so it could immediately generate conversation.

"Therefore, if you do not really have another preference, I would recommend you to take this maxi dress," concluded Scarlett.

After hearing all the analysis, Ruth also came to see that the maxi dress was better, and eventually bought it from Scarlett.

In the above story, Scarlett gave Ruth a lot of information about the dresses, such as the designs that were the most popular and their various advantages. However, you will not have found it at all confusing, and you are likely to feel that you have learned a lot of things from her. In order to understand how she managed that, let us consider a little memory exercise below.

The Limit of Human Memory

Here is a little mental exercise for you. You are going to see a list of 12 words. Look at the list for 10 seconds, then look away and recall as many words as possible. Here is the list:

- Bow

- China

- Durian

- Axe

- Cherry

- Denmark

- Aruba

- Banana

- Club

- Apple

- Dagger

- Brazil

How many words can you recall? Not many people can remember more than half of them after looking at the list for 10 seconds. Now let me point out that there are actually four sets of three words that start with the same letter, like this:

- A:

  ○ Axe

  ○ Apple

  ○ Aruba

- B:

- Banana
- Brazil
- Bow
- **C:**
- China
- Cherry
- Club
- **D:**
- Durian
- Denmark
- Dagger

Now try to repeat the exercise. How many can you recall now? Most people can do much better this time. Now let me give you one more tip: in each of the four groups above, there is a fruit, a weapon and a country. Now look at the list again:

- **A: Apple, Axe, Aruba**

- B: Banana, Bow, Brazil

- C: Cherry, Club, China

- D: Durian, Dagger, Denmark

Now try to recall the words one more time. After the regrouping, most people will find it easier to recall the words, because the regrouping reduced the number of things that you have to remember. Originally, there were 12 separate words to memorise, but after the regrouping process, you only have to remember two things: one, there are four alphabets, and two, there are three object types. As long as you remember these two features, you can easily remind yourself what the original words are.

Therefore, if you can simplify your information into just a few categories, your listener will find it easier to remember. In the story, Scarlett also used a similar method of simplification to help her customer to choose a ballroom dress, and the process could be broken down into the following two steps.

First, she selected the best options for the customer to consider. One of the most important values of an expert is the ability to digest complex information into just a few important points. Ladies' fashion is always full of different styles and designs, and with so many choices, the customers always want an expert to quickly pick a few best ones for them, without their having to go through all the possibilities themselves. By immediately distilling the best choices into just two styles, Scarlett was able to save the customer a great deal of time in pondering the lesser choices.

Then Scarlett went on to analyse which one was more suitable for Ruth. Here she provided two perspectives: body shape and social function. After going through each criterion, she finally concluded that Ruth should have the maxi dress instead of the other one. It showed the customer that her recommendation was based on careful consideration of many factors, and thus it was objective and reliable.

In conclusion, the above process could be summarised as the Three C's:

1 Categorise: what are the choices?

2 Characterise: what are they about?

3 Criticise: which one is the best?

It is a very good way to present your ideas to your listeners, because you can summarise things into just a few key points for them to digest. However, you may wonder: if you really want to simplify your presentation, why do you have to present two choices instead of simply mentioning the best one?

The Good and the Bad

Suppose there are two financial advisers who come to see you, and both of them want to persuade you to buy an equity fund that invests in emerging Asian countries. The first one tells you:

"The GDP of the Asian countries grew by 10 per cent last year. Moreover, most of the Asian countries are not as debt-ridden as their Western counterparts. Therefore, if you want to invest for the long term, this is the place for you."

The second adviser tells you:

"When we look for a certain country or collection of countries to invest in, we usually have to consider two factors. The first one is the economic growth of the area, so that the stronger its growth, the better the prospect it ensures. The second thing is the national debt of the countries, because a lower debt level often means less sovereign risk.

"In terms of growth, the emerging Asian countries are definitely a good buy because their GDP grew by 10 per cent last year, which is higher than any other region. These countries are also not as debt-ridden as some of their Western counterparts such as Spain or Italy. In either case, it is not unreasonable to consider investing in the emerging Asian markets. Therefore, if you want to invest for the long term, this is the place for you."

Which adviser do you find more convincing? Most people are more likely to listen to the second adviser. The main difference between the two is that, while the first adviser only focuses on introducing the advantages of the Asian market (i.e. the thing he wants to sell), the second adviser makes a detailed comparison between the Asian market and other areas before he presents his conclusion. By doing so, the second adviser gives the impression that he is not hard-selling you any particular product, and his conclusion is fair and objective.

In addition to that, the second adviser is also able to provide you with more insights into the financial market. By offers two key factors to consider (GDP growth and debt level), the second adviser teaches the client how to analyse the global economy in a simple way. This is a very important skill, because customers often admire advisers who can explain them the most important things in an easy-to-understand way. This is possibly one of the fastest ways to build trust with the customers.

It is similar in Scarlett's story. If she had only recommended the maxi dress to Ruth without making a comparison with the other one, it would have been less convincing. Therefore, she had to first divide the best choices into a few categories, then compare them. More formally, this process is called a dichotomisation, which is a systematic process of organising data into different categories. One example of its application is in biology, where organisms are classified into many different types, to make it easier to study them.

Here is something interesting to note: each time Scarlett used a dichotomisation, she limited the number of categories to just two. When she suggested Ruth what to wear, she only gave her two choices; and when she explained which one was better for her, she also only mentioned two reasons. Why did she always just stick to the number of two?

Keep It Simple, Sir

As explained earlier, the idea of dichotomisation is to aid our memory by organising data into a small number of categories, so that the fewer categories there are, the easier it is for people to remember them. This is why Scarlett stuck with only two categories each time, because it is the way to ensure maximum simplicity in her presentation.

However, sometimes you cannot avoid using more than two categories. If that is really the case, the best idea is to limit them to no more than three, because once you get above this number, you may overload your listeners with too much information, and make them feel uncomfortable. Nevertheless, what if you really have a lot to say, making it necessary to use more than three categories?

In that case, you should ask yourself two questions. First, is there any information that is not really important? Try to delete any redundant information to simplify what you have to say. You will often find that you have included too many trifles, which will not be very interesting to your listeners.

Still, if you really believe that it is impossible to cut out anything, then ask yourself a second question: is it possible to chunk them up into bigger categories?

For example, suppose you want to mention that there are six continents in the world: Asia, Europe, Australasia, Africa, and North and South America. One way to simplify your presentation is to group them into just three categories: America, Euro-Africa, and Asia-Pacific. After that, you can break each category down into subdivisions. It can make your presentation much more succinct and lucid.

In conclusion, the technique of dichotomisation is one of the best ways to impress your audience, because they can learn a lot of new information from you in a clear and simple manner as though you are their teacher. However, while this is certainly a very valuable technique, there is a still more powerful trick that can win the hearts of your listeners even faster, by using as examples the most influential figures in history.

The Power of Superstition

Queen Elizabeth I, Napoleon Bonaparte and Adolf Hitler are three very prominent people in history. Elizabeth I was a great English monarch who is regarded as the ruler of a golden age, and defended her country against a Spanish invasion. Napoleon was a brilliant military genius who built up a powerful empire, and exercised great domestic and foreign influence. For Hitler, even though he is possibly the coarsest and cruellest dictator ever, he was instrumental in turning Germany from a ravaged and heavily indebted mess into a world power in a very short time.

Apart than their historical fame, they share another common characteristic: they were three of the most superstitious people in history. Elizabeth I had a magician, John Dee, who helped her in making decisions with regards to state affairs. Napoleon consulted with a clairvoyant, Madame Normand, when he required advice for his war campaigns. Adolf Hitler was known to seek advice from both astrologers and fortune tellers, and was insanely superstitious about the potency of the number seven.

Why do people as potent and brilliant as them believe in something so silly? The truth is: even great people can be easily influenced. Soothsayers usually use a language pattern that can create a false impression of omniscience in their clients – no matter whether the clients are average people in the street, millionaires who run multinational businesses, or even the most influential leaders in history. What had the fortune tellers said to make these people trust them so much? And can you apply the same skills to your customers? The answers to these two questions will be found in the next chapter.

3. Prophetic Predictions

How to Look More Mature?

One day, when Scarlett was working in the boutique as usual, she found a young woman looking around the shop. When Scarlett saw her, she noticed that she was different from most of the customers that she normally saw.

Usually, these were university girls who dressed in a very fashionable and stylish manner. However, this young woman did not only dress in pale colours, but also wore plain glasses. Clearly, she was not short-sighted, and she was only wearing them for her look. In addition to that, Scarlett discovered a blue stain on her shirt.

Scarlett went up to her and asked: "Hi there. Are you looking for anything?"

"Thanks. Nothing in particular, perhaps just some clothes for work," she replied in a polite manner.

"I see. I find that you dress in a special way. You must be working in a job related to education," said Scarlett.

"I am a teacher. How can you know that?" The customer was surprised.

"Well, we people working in the fashion industry are very observant about the way one dresses," said Scarlett. "Normally teachers wear loosely fitted but well-tailored clothes, and they wear glasses to make themselves look more mature," said Scarlett.

"Oh, that is amazing!" claimed the woman.

"Thank you. However, I observed that there is also a relatively new spot of blue ink on your shirt. You must have gone through some trouble recently."

"Oh yes!" said the customer. "My class made me angry today. I accidentally knocked the ink pad off, and it fell on to me. Luckily, the spot is not too big."

"I suspect you often feel that your class do not respect you as much as they should?"

"Yes, my colleagues said I look too young, which is why I wear these lenses. However, apparently it doesn't help much."

"Forgive me, but I am not surprised that it would not help," said Scarlett suddenly.

"What do you mean?" asked the teacher.

"The problem does not lie in the glasses, but in your clothes," said Scarlett. "To look more experienced, there are two things to which you must pay attention. Firstly, the colours of your clothes should not be too pale, because this does not give a solid sense of feeling. Secondly, they need to have a rich texture, which can make you look mature. Although what you are wearing is certainly appropriate for work, it does not inspire confidence."

"Then what should I do?" The teacher seemed concerned.

"Don't worry. Please come this way, and I will show you some clothes that can help you."

Then Scarlett gave the teacher a dress and let her put it on in the fitting room. After that, Scarlett asked her:

"What do you find most impressive about this dress?"

"Well, I do look more mature in it."

"That's true. You have a petite body, and for your body size there are usually two ways to look more mature. You could either wear gender-neutral clothes, or traditional clothes with refined colours. Since you are a teacher, the first option is not really viable. This dress has a classical design which projects an impression of maturity."

"I see. I do like this dress a lot."

"However, there is one more reason why this dress can work for you."

"Really? Could you tell me what that is?"

"We usually spend more as we have more income. Do you find that since you graduated from uni and got a job, you have spent more money on clothing than when you were studying?"

"Yes, I think I have."

"In general, when you were young and had no income, you could only afford cheap things. However, as you earn more money, you often want to improve the quality of your clothing. Therefore, the best way to avoid looking young is to avoid cheap clothes and put on something of a higher quality.

"But of course, we don't want to look posh. We look for clothes that are of high quality but still adequate for schools. While this dress belongs to the high-quality category, it is still traditional enough for a teacher. When people see you wearing it, they will think that you must be a mature person."

The teacher laughed, "I certainly hope so!"

"However, I will still ask you to think carefully before you buy it," said Scarlett.

"Why's that?" asked the teacher.

"According to my experience, most women often buy a lot of clothes, but never wear them again. Do you have a lot of clothes in your wardrobe that you seldom wear?"

"Yes I do."

"That being said, I would like to tell you that you do not have to worry about this dress. I am sure it will be useful for a long time."

"And why are you so sure?"

"There are two reasons for that," said Scarlet. "Firstly, it is about the quality. If the quality is poor, it will soon get damaged. However, this dress is of high quality, so it can survive a long time.

"Secondly, it is about its use. If the dress is only for special occasions, then you will not wear it very often. On the other hand, if it is for work, then you will surely wear it every day."

"I see what you mean," said the teacher.

"If you buy it elsewhere in the bigger shops, it will be more expensive than getting it here. Therefore, if you really feel that this dress is suitable for you, and if you really want to look more mature when you work, I believe you can seriously consider it," said Scarlett.

Eventually, the teacher bought the dress from Scarlett.

Artfully Vague

This is a book on the art of persuasion, and people who read this kind of book usually share some common characteristics. You are in a situation in life in which you hope to achieve something that is essential to you. You really want to minimise the resistance and difficulties that you will face, and make your journey smooth and easy.

Unfortunately, life is often not that straightforward. In fact, you cannot remember how many times you have screwed up a situation that is really important. Sometimes, you just cannot imagine how wrong things can go, and you really want to curse the whole world because you are really disappointed. Even though you always try your best to go after what you want, sometimes you just feel that lady luck is not smiling on you.

Nevertheless, you are a person with considerable strength, and you always have a good instinct to do the right things. Sometimes, you have a strong gut feeling which points you in the right direction, and causes you to discover new possibilities. Sadly, you often give in to your laziness and doubt, and avoid taking actions as a result. Very often you will later regret that you have missed a good chance to go after what you want.

Does that sound like you? If it does, then I would like to let you know that I actually know nothing about you at all. It is nothing more than a technique known as cold reading.

Cold reading is a verbal trick which creates an impression that the speaker knows a lot about the listeners, when in fact the speaker actually does not. This trick usually utilises a language pattern which is best described as "artfully vague." It means that the content is vague enough to mean virtually anything, so that each listener could assign a different meaning to it. In other words, it is up to the listeners to decide what the words in the speech are supposed to mean, and hence it makes it look as though the speaker can read their minds.

The passage above is a typical example of cold reading. Even though it looks as though I have said a lot of things, the meaning is so universal that it can actually mean anything. For instance, look at this sentence: "You are in a situation in life in which you hope to achieve something that is essential to you." What exactly is that essential thing? How essential is that, and in what way? It did not specify at all. When you read that, your mind immediately retrieves something from your memory that could be considered "essential" to fill in the blanks. After all, who does not have something which he considers "essential" to achieve?

Cold reading is a very effective skill to create a false façade of omniscience, and it is extensively used by people such as bogus fortune tellers and astrologers to fool their customers. Consider this typical piece of horoscope which you can often see in newspapers:

"Worries about your fortune could plague you today. Someone who is very close to you could have given you some doubtful information about your financial situation recently. Most likely, it is regarding rumours in your life that could affect your finances. Don't waste time worrying. Check out the facts before driving yourself crazy. You will probably find that you've been misinformed."

If you are a clerk who has been dabbling in the stock market, you will think: "Yes! My friend has given me a tip to buy a mining company in Australia. He said that the company has just secured a very important contract with China, but I am not sure yet. I have been thinking about it for days."

If you are a young housewife who has never invested in anything before, you will still think that it is accurate: "That is true! My friend is persuading me to open a new account in a small bank. She said they are doing a promotion for new customers, and offer a very high fixed deposit rate. However, there is a rumour that the bank is having some managerial problems itself, so I am still thinking about it."

Or even if you are just a schoolboy, you can still think that it is true, "My mother always give me pocket money every Sunday. However, yesterday someone in the school accused me of stealing a watch. My mother said she will not give me any money until the school finds out what happened. I cannot buy anything now."

Why does everyone find the horoscope true? It is simply because terms like "financial situation" and "rumours" are vague enough to mean virtually anything. Is your investment a financial situation? Of course it is. Is doing a fixed deposit in a bank a financial situation? No doubt. Is your pocket money from your parents also a financial situation? Indeed. No matter who is reading this, the reader can always find something that fits the description.

It can also happen in a face-to-face session of fortune telling. For example, when you go to see a fortune teller sitting behind a crystal ball, she can tell you:

"I see a strange spirit hovering around you. Do you live with someone else?"

"Yes, I've just moved in with my new husband."

"Is it a very sweet home?"

"Yes it is!"

"Oh, that is it. This is a spirit of blessing and good fortune. You are going to see more happy things in the next three months. Let me do a more in-depth reading with you to see how to make the most out of it."

On the other hand, what will happen if you answer otherwise? Suppose you tell her: "No, I live alone." What will she say?

She can still continue to probe you: "Are you in love with anyone?"

"No, I am still single."

"You mean you have never dated anyone before?"

"I have. I have dated three times before, but it broke up in the end each time."

"I see. This is a spirit of loneliness. It is the reason why you have failed in your relationships and are now living alone. If you do not drive it away, it will continue to haunt you. Why don't you let me do an in-depth reading for you to see how to get rid of it?"

No matter what you say, the fortune teller can always appear to be correct, and the innocent souls will really believe that they have supernatural powers that can guide them to success. While it looks incredible, it is actually a trick that can be learned by everyone.

How to Become a Prophet

In the above example, the fortune teller appears to know about everything that has happened to the listener. Of course, as explained earlier, she actually knows nothing. To understand how she does it, you can break down the conversation into three parts:

1 First, she gives you an artfully vague statement which could mean anything: "There is a spirit hovering around you." However, the fortune teller does not specify what kind of spirit it is, and what effect it has on you.

2 Then she starts to ask you more questions to probe into your situation: "Are you living with anyone?" "I live with my husband." "Are you happy together?" "Yes." Through this conversation the fortune teller gains a lot of actual information about you.

3 With this information, she relates the "spirit" she talked about to your actual situation. If you say that you are happy, then she will tell you: "This is a spirit of blessing and fortune," and vice versa. It makes her look as though she really can predict your future.

In summary, what the fortune teller does can be summarised into three simple steps. For the sake of mnemonic convenience, each step has a name that starts with the letter "B":

1 Babble: Talk with "artfully vague" words.

2 Burrow: Inquire into the specific situation.

3 Boast: Reaffirm yourself by showing off.

You can also apply this skill of cold reading in any everyday situation to make yourself look like a prophet. Let us go back to the story of Scarlett at the beginning of the chapter. In the story, Scarlett made a series of predictions about the customer, such as that she was a teacher, and that the class did not listen to her, and so on. Every time she did that, she also followed the method of the three B's. Let us consider them one by one.

Here is the first cold reading. When the teacher entered the shop, Scarlett observed that what she wore was very close to the attire of an education worker. So she began:

1 Babble: "You dress in a very special way." Can a statement be vaguer than that?

2 Burrow: "You must work in a job related to education." And it turned out that Scarlett had guessed correctly. The teacher was surprised that she knew her occupation.

3 Boast: After guessing it correctly, Scarlett reaffirmed herself: "Well, we people working in the fashion industry are very observant about the way one dresses. Normally teachers wear loosely fitted but well-tailored clothes." It made the teacher believed that she really knew something about fashion.

In this case, you can see that Scarlett was luckily right that she was a teacher. Of course, you may start to wonder: "What if she was not a teacher?" We will come back to this question later. Until then, let us go back to the story.

The second cold reading of the story began when she saw a blue stain on the shirt of the customer:

1 Babble: "I observed that there is also a relatively new spot of blue ink on your shirt. You must have gone through some trouble recently." Please note that Scarlett did not say what kind of trouble and how it happened. A bit of common sense can tell you that no one deliberately makes her own clothes dirty, so it must have been by some accident.

2 Burrow: The teacher went on to tell her that her class had made her angry on that day, so she had accidentally knocked an ink pad off the desk. Scarlett went on to surmise that the class did not listen to her very often, and she was right again. Lucky enough for her, the teacher expressed the desire to look more mature. Scarlett then seized the opportunity.

3 Boast: Scarlett then redirected the teacher's attention to her attire: "The problem does not lie in the glasses, but in your clothes." Then she went on to explain how to look more mature. Here she employed the dichotomisation trick from the last chapter, and explained that there were two things to which the

teacher must pay attention. It immediately made her looked very knowledgeable in dressing.

The third cold reading came after the teacher had put on the dress in the fitting room:

1 Babble: Scarlett lured the teacher to try on a dress by saying: "Although what you are wearing is certainly appropriate for work, it does not inspire confidence." Note that here Scarlett was implying a distorted logic: you do not look confident enough because you do not dress well, so that if you want to look confident, you should buy something here.

2 Burrow: After the teacher put on the dress, she asked her, "What do you find most impressive about this dress?" And the teacher agreed that the dress did make her look more mature. Note that Scarlett asked the question in a very clever way. She did not ask her, "Do you like the dress?" If the teacher had said no, she would have had a long way to get back on track. Instead, she made a presupposition that the teacher already liked the dress, and asked her what she found most impressive about it. It made her focus on the positive things.

3 Boast: "That's true. You have a petite body, and for this body size there are usually two ways to look more mature." Again, she demonstrated her expertise on attire by the dichotomisation trick.

Scarlett went on with another cold reading as she continued to sell the dress:

1 Babble: "We usually spend more as we have more income." Well, who doesn't spend more as they earn more? It is always a good way to begin a cold reading by referring to some universal experience like this one, because no one can argue against it.

2 Burrow: "Do you find that since you graduated from uni and started working you have spent more money on clothing than when you were studying?" The teacher gave an affirmative response.

3 Boast: Scarlett went on to explain how the dress could help her to look mature, and again she used the dichotomisation trick to aid her explanation.

At last, Scarlett closed the deal with a final cold reading:

1 Babble: "According to my experience, most women often buy a lot of clothes but never wear them again." Again, it is a universal experience – most people buy more things than they actually need, and end up storing a lot of useless things at home.

2 Burrow: "Do you have a lot of clothes in your wardrobe that you seldom wear?" And the teacher did.

3 Boast: "I would like to tell you that you do not have to worry about this dress." And Scarlett went on to explain why the dress would last a long time, and be of frequent use to her.

The reason that Scarlett mentioned this point was that she wanted to handle some possible rejections in advance. Usually, when you have to buy something that is not cheap, you are likely to worry about whether you really need it. By reaffirming the usefulness of the dress, Scarlett had effectively dealt with two very common reasons for rejection: too expensive, and may not need it. It made the closing of the deal much easier.

This skill of cold reading looks very magical and effective. However, as mentioned earlier, you may not guess right all the time. What happens if you unfortunately guess it wrong? The answer is: it really does not matter whether you guess it right or wrong, because you can still demonstrate your expertise, regardless of the response.

I Am Always Right

Let us return to the story of Scarlett above. Suppose the customer had told Scarlett at the beginning: "I am not a teacher. I am an admin staff in the City Hall nearby." What would you say if you were her?

If you wanted to reply, "Sorry, I made a mistake," then you are not professional enough to be a super salesman. Instead, Scarlett would have said:

"I see. You dress in a very polite and gentle manner, which is common for conservative workplaces like schools or the government. I think your glasses also make you look elegant."

And the customer might reply:

"Thank you. Indeed, I am very conscious about my appearance, and that is why I wear glasses, even though my eyesight is normal."

"Talking about appearance, I cannot help but to notice that there is a relatively new blue stain on your shirt. Perhaps there was some trouble at work?"

"Not really! I have just been promoted and have got a raise. When I got the news today, I was so happy that I accidentally knocked the ink pad off the desk, and it fell onto my clothes. Fortunately, the spot is not too big."

"I think the people at work must like you very much."

"Well, let's just say we are working very well together."

"I don't find it surprising, because you dress very elegantly. It must have left a very good impression on everyone in the office."

"Thank you. In fact, there is no one in my office who cares about their appearance as much as me."

"Indeed. I find that the colours of your shirt and glasses go very well together, so that it gives you a very coherent look."

"Yes, it took me some time to mix and match."

"When it comes to mix and match, I think there is a good jacket that will go very well with what you are wearing today. Why don't you come over here and try it on, and see how well it will work out for you?"

So you see, no matter what the other person answers, you can always demonstrate your expert knowledge. In this new example, Scarlett almost guessed wrong every time, but she still somehow managed to get around it, and eventually persuaded the customer to try on some clothes. This is why you should always start your cold reading with an "artfully vague" statement that provides enough room for you to manoeuvre after you have gone wrong.

Doing a cold reading requires a fine balance between being vague and specific. If you are vague all the time, then it will just look like a horoscope. On the other hand, if you are too cocksure right from the start, then it is hard to circumvent embarrassment when you get it wrong. This is why you should alternate between vague and concrete statements. In the beginning, try to be vague to avoid mistakes. When you are lucky enough to be right, you can immediately be more specific by boasting about your knowledge, and then go back to the vague mode again to ask for more information.

Nevertheless, you still cannot avoid guessing wrong every now and then. What should you do if you have got it wrong? The first thing to do is not to panic. The whole point of doing a cold reading is to appear authoritative, so it will defeat the whole purpose if you appear panicky or apologise too soon. The next thing you should do is to identify the kind of customers that you are facing.

In general, there are two kinds of customers: the confident ones and the self-doubting ones. In the new version of Scarlett's story, the customer is obviously very confident about the way she dresses, so she belongs to the first kind. When you meet this kind of customer, you should praise whatever she has done well, and encourage her to go on talking. In the story, Scarlett praised the customer for looking elegant, and the customer was delighted, so that they went on to have a conversation – which kept selling opportunities open.

It is even simpler if your customer belongs to the self-doubting category. If there is an obvious defect or weakness in your customer, then you can home in on that and demonstrate your knowledge. Suppose the customer in Scarlett's story had answered her, "No, I am actually a marketing officer in a media company." Obviously, it is not quite right for a marketing officer to dress like a teacher, so Scarlett could have criticised her, and gone on to show off her knowledge.

Of course, you should keep in mind that you don't want to come across as rude when you criticise your listener. The purpose of doing all these is not to offend him, but to show off what you know. In short, whenever you have guessed wrong, praise or criticise your listener accordingly, so that you can demonstrate your knowledge either way.

Some people may think that all these are a bit unnecessary, and they may think, "This is all very interesting. However, I am a very candid person and I don't like to play games like that. Why can't I just tell people what I know directly?" Well, there are actually two very important reasons of why you should follow the method of the three B's instead of telling them directly.

The Merit of Asking More

Imagine that the teacher in the story entered another boutique instead of the one in which Scarlett worked. A salesgirl there also noticed that she dressed conservatively and wore plain lenses. However, this time, the salesgirl told the teacher immediately: "We have a very nice dress that is very suitable for teachers. Would you like to have a look?"

Surely the teacher would have the following feelings:

1 I did not ask for your opinion, why bother?

2 Do you mean I don't look like a teacher now?

3 You are just trying to sell me the dress.

Let us look at another example. Suppose you have just entered a pharmacy, and a salesman there tries to sell you a certain kind of blueberry pills. If he goes into it directly by saying:

"Blueberry pills are very good for eyes and they can improve night vision. They contain an extract called lutein, which maintains a healthy macula and prevents retinal degeneration."

Put this way, you will not see anything special about the pills that will make you feel you must buy them. Now try to compare the above with the following. The salesman starts by asking, "Are you short-sighted?"

"Slightly," you answer.

"Have you ever found that your eyes sometimes get tired very easily? Yet there are also times when you can look at the computer screen for a long time without any problem?"

"Yes, I have experienced that."

"This is because our eyes need a substance called lutein to maintain their function. When your eyes get enough lutein, they don't feel tired – even after a long time – and vice versa. By the way, lutein is also useful to prevent the deepening of myopia. If you want a good lutein supplement, you should try these blueberry pills."

The point of doing a series of cold readings is to give your customer the evidence to believe that you are an expert in what he is looking for, as well as an opportunity for you to demonstrate why he needs your product. In other words, it provides the necessary grounding for him to develop confidence in you, as well as the logical reasons for why your product is necessary for him.

Another reason for doing all these is to avoid coming across as too hard-selling. Suppose one day you are chatting with a friend who knows a lot about computers. You tell him that you have just bought a new tablet computer made by Company A, and he tells you, "Oh, Company A's tablets are not as good as those of Company B, and Company A is famous for selling overpriced stuff."

Then you tell him that it was not too expensive because you got it with a 20 per cent discount. He replies, "But Company B's tablets have more functions than Company A's."

You let him know that you are not very computer-savvy, so just the basic functions are enough for you. This time he says, "Even so, Company B's are more user-friendly for beginners."

Do you find him a bit annoying? No matter what you say, he always immediately comes back with something which proves you an idiot. Even if everything he says is true, you will still be reluctant to listen to him. Now imagine your friend says it in a different way. After you tell him about buying a new computer, he says:

"I heard that Company A's tablets are not cheap at all."

"Yes, even after a 20 per cent discount, I still don't think they are cheap."

"That is why I often just buy from Company B. It is cheaper and has more functions. Does the Internet browser of your tablet support Flash?"

"No, it does not."

"You see? The Company A's tablets are not as useful as Company B's. They are actually less user-friendly as well."

In this version, he delays his real response by asking you a few questions first, and only comes back to his point after he hears you. In this way, he not only prevents himself from looking obnoxious, but also gives you an impression that he is listening to you. The question-and-answering of the 3B's method serves the same purpose, so that you appear to be having a meaningful conversation with your customer – when you are, in fact, selling to him.

However, no matter how well you can conduct a conversation, it is useless to you if you do not know how to approach a customer to start with. In business, there are only two situations: either the customer finds you, or you find the customer. In the former case, it is very easy to start a conversation with him, because the customer has already expressed the need. However, most of the time, it is the other way round.

Have you ever experienced something like the following? You enter a retail store just to browse around without looking for anything specifically. Then a salesman in the store pops up and asks, "Do you need any help?" You reply, "Thanks, just browsing." And then you find that the salesman tries to follow you around, possibly to strike up a conversation in order to create selling opportunities. Since you are not really interested in talking to him, it slightly annoys you and you get out of the shop immediately. In the end, the shop loses a customer, and you do not have time to look for what you want.

The more experienced salespeople usually adopt a very different approach. They will not even bother to ask you, "Do you need any help?" because they know you will probably say no. So what might they do instead? You will learn it in the next chapter.

4. Instant Attention

A Very Bad Cold Call

One day, while I was writing this book, I received a call from a financial brokerage for gold trading. As soon as I answered the call, the girl on the other side of the phone asked if I knew anything about the gold market. Since I am also a salesman, I sometimes like to listen to other cold-callers to see if I can learn a few things as well, so I pretended that I was interested in what she was selling.

Once I asked her to go on, she launched into her pitch, and talked about all the technical details about gold trading for almost two minutes, such as how to go long and short, how to calculate profits and so on. However, her presentation was really boring, so that even after three minutes or so, I still did not hear anything that could interest me.

Normally, I would have already hung up, but I thought it would make a good material for this book, so I decided to interrupt her.

"So what has that to do with me?" I asked.

"Sorry?"

"In which ways do you think gold trading is going to benefit me?"

"Gold trading helps you because..." and she restated what she had been talking about in the previous two or three minutes – i.e. reciting boring information that interested no one.

I could not help but to interrupt again: "But why do you think gold will go up again?"

"Well, because we have flat money and inflation, it will mean that gold prices will keep going higher."

After hearing that, I challenged her: "The US has been printing money since the Seventies, but why has gold never increased much during this long period?"

A tone of exasperation crept into her voice: "Well, because the demand for gold is increasing. Anyway, the trend in gold prices is still going up, so it is still a good way to make profit…"

Once again, the salesperson went into the technical details of gold trading. By that time, I didn't feel like keeping her on the line any longer, so I said, "I am sorry, but I don't feel interested in your service at the moment."

After a significant pause, she said, "Sorry to bother you," and she hung up.

I have no doubt that she was a bit disappointed, but so was I. To be honest, she was a really poor salesperson. I had already given her five full minutes to prove herself, but she was still unable to arouse my interest in such a long period, and it was a very, very fatal mistake for a salesman.

How Much Is Patience Worth?

People always say that patience is a virtue. Benjamin Franklin once said, "He that can have patience can have what he will." However, in the modern world of communication, you no longer need patience to get what you will, because digital technology has facilitated access to information to an unprecedented level of convenience, so that all the "patience" you need could be just as little as a few seconds.

When you look at the statistics, you will find some very surprising results. A 2011 website usage study showed that an Internet user in the United Kingdom visits as many as 2,518 web pages across 81 domains within 53 sessions in one single month. In other words, you no longer need to ring your doctor friend to ask for information about medicine. Instead, just a few clicks on Google and Wikipedia will do. Unfortunately, while this increases our efficiency in research, it also has some undesirable effects.

An Internet study in the States in 2012 suggested that, while students benefit from instant access to a wealth of information from numerous sources, their attention span and desire for in-depth analysis is consequently diminished. The report pointed out that the current generation of Internet consumers lives in a world of "instant gratification", which leads to a "loss of patience and a lack of deep thinking."

With such an overload of information, people are becoming more and more impatient towards anything that cannot catch their attention quickly. Researchers find that, for classified advertisements, less than one in five readers read on from the headlines – which means that you will miss more than 80 per cent of your readers if you do not write a good headline. The very first line of your message decides the fate of your advertisement.

It is the same with online marketing. Studies about internet marketing have shown that 32 per cent of consumers abandon slow sites in one to five seconds. In addition, a one-second delay in page-load time can result in 11 per cent fewer page views, 16 per cent decreased customer satisfaction and 7 per cent lost conversions. Every second counts! People are busy, and if you cannot prove yourself in a few seconds, then you are out.

This is why advertisements always use different ways to catch your attention as soon as possible. Advertisements in media always include elements such as catchy music, sexy people, visual humour and emotive words, because all these appeal to our basic sensory perceptions, and it is the most efficient way to get your attention in the fastest way possible.

This is the same for face-to-face selling. When you approach a prospect, you must make him interested as soon as possible, so that he is willing to give you more time to continue, instead of turning away. In other words, the success (or failure) of a sales process is already decided as soon as the very first minute. Unfortunately, just like the gold-trading girl in the above story, most salespeople are unable to put this knowledge into practice.

Attention Is Scarce

Most salespeople believe in a brutal approach in finding prospects. They just use the same old repeated lines to hit on one person after another, hopeful that one day they will bump into someone who is interested in their products. To some extent, it is like playing a slot machine in a casino: you constantly insert your coins into the machine, and hope that eventually you will hit the jackpot.

You may argue that those people working in a large institution have to follow a predetermined script written by their company, so they cannot improvise their openings when they approach their customers on the phone. If that is the case, we can consider another example: job interviews.

A job interview often begins when the interviewer asks the candidate to introduce himself. For 99 per cent of the candidates, their self-introduction goes like this.

"I have just graduated from the University of Cambridge in Economics, where I got first-class honours. During my second year, I was the president of the Business School Club, where we held many events for business leaders of tomorrow. Besides that, I also worked as an intern in the Royal Bank of Scotland to familiarise myself with the internal operation of a bank."

To be fair, this is a very clear self-introduction, which outlines the most important aspects of the candidate. And surely enough, the credentials of the candidate are not too bad. However, from a professional point of view, this candidate has already made as many as three major mistakes in this very short introduction.

You see, if you want to succeed in job interviews, you must realise that interviewers are very busy people who have a lot of other things to do apart from interviewing you. If they are qualified to interview you, then they must be at least in the middle level of management, and have many other tasks to finish. To them, half an hour of time could be used to do a lot of work, so using the same amount of time to interview a candidate is a great cost to them.

Given these conditions, what attitude do you think they will adopt when they interview you?

They will try to finish it as soon as possible, of course. They would rather save energy to do their own things, instead of wasting time to chat with an uninteresting person. They will try to get an impression of the candidate in the most efficient manner, and if he is not up to what they want, they will send him away and get back to work as soon as possible.

Therefore, interviewers can make hiring decisions as early as the first five minutes of the interview. If one likes you from the start, then you will be able to keep your chances alive. On the other hand, if you cannot impress him in the first few minutes, then no matter how competent you actually are, the interviewer will never be interested in finding out.

Going back to the interview example we have just read, what mistakes does the candidate make in his self-introduction? Let's count:

Mistake 1: It's interesting, but not enough.

The candidate points out the most significant facts about him, but facts are far from enough to create interest. As seen in the gold trading cold call example, the salesgirl had told me everything about gold trading, but she was unable to capture my interest in that. In order to create interest, you must include some intriguing statements to make them go on asking questions.

Mistake 2: The interviewer has to do the work.

Following the last point, if you cannot bring out the most interesting things about yourself, then the interviewer will be forced to do the work and find them out. In a good job interview, the interviewer is merely an audience in a theatre, who is simply sitting there to enjoy your performance. It is completely different in a bad interview. If the candidate is unable to present himself, the interviewer will suddenly become the director, and tell the candidate what to tell him.

Mistake 3: It conveys no value to the interviewer.

In layman's term, he does not make himself look useful after the introduction. To be fair, he does mention that he comes from Cambridge and runs the business club, which are supposed to be his selling points. However, how could those things help you in the position for which you are applying now? It was left unexplained.

Of course, it is easier to point out a problem than to provide a solution. So how can the above candidate improve his self-introduction? Let us consider the following story of Mr. Kyle Thomson, the retired fashion designer mentioned in the first chapter.

Horror on the Orient Express

As a retired fashion designer who had worked in France for a number of years, Mr. Kyle Thomson had a few connections there. One day, he was invited by a former colleague to a fashion show in Paris, and he gladly accepted the invitation. However, when he arrived at Roissy airport in Paris, he encountered something interesting.

Since Mr. Thomson had arrived early in the morning, more than an hour before the arrival of his coach, he decided to have a bit of breakfast first in a café in the airport. While he was eating, he heard some people talking at the next table:

"Have you heard about the news about that Budapest incident?" asked one of them.

"Yes, someone was assaulted on a luxury train in Budapest. Is that what you're talking about?" replied the other person.

"Yes, I heard that he is a political figure from an African country. Do you know who he is?"

"No, but I hear that he is a very radical character, and he is the leader of some extreme political movement in his country."

Suddenly, an African man from another table joined in the conversation.

"Yes, he is. I am from the same country as his. He is a very charismatic bloke. He is fighting for democracy in our country. My father-in-law is an ardent supporter of his."

"Oh really, can you tell us what's his name?"

"Of course, his name is... oh what is it? It's just slipped my mind. Let me think... wait a minute, what time is it now?"

"It's half six."

"Oh no, my coach will be departing soon. Anyway, it's been nice talking to you!"

"You too, have a nice day!"

And the African man went away. Mr. Thomson was curious about the Budapest news they were talking about. It was a pity that he had no access to the Internet. If he had not been in a foreign country he could have immediately checked it on his smart phone.

Ten minutes later, Mr. Thomson saw another customer entering the cafe.

"Good morning, would you like anything?" asked the waitress.

"Yes, a tall latte please," replied the customer. "I need a cup of coffee to cheer myself up after reading some horrible news.

"Oh," replied the waitress, "You mean that incident in Budapest?"

"What? It's that again?" Mr. Thomson wondered.

"Yes, I've just checked the news in the Internet corner in your café. How horrible it is! They say that if he dies there could be a war in Africa!"

"Wow, really? Can it be so serious?" said the waitress.

Mr. Thomson also began to wonder about it. What was this mysterious incident all about? Suddenly, he thought it would be a good idea to check out the news like that man had done, so he stood up from the table and went straight to the Internet corner.

However, as he approached the computer he then realised that his coach would be departing in a few minutes, so he got the bill, hurried out of the café and dashed towards the coach station.

The Mysterious Freedom Fighter

Since he hadn't slept on the plane, Mr. Thomson was quite tired. As soon as he sat down on the coach, he closed his eyes and tried to take a nap. As he was relaxing, he heard the people sitting on the opposite side of the aisle say:

"Hey, you know about the African politician in Budapest?"

"No, what is it about?"

"He is in a very dangerous condition! He may die soon!"

"What? The same man I heard about earlier?" thought Mr. Thomson. He wanted to join the conversation but he was too tired.

"So why should I care if he dies?" asked one of them on the other side.

"Well, he has a lot of supporters in his country, if he really does die, then it is possible that there will be civil war there."

"Will it? Why is that?"

"Because he is the leader of a democratic movement in his country. It annoys the dictator so much that the existing government wants to eliminate him."

"And what is the name of that politician?"

"Oh, let me see, his name is..."

Unfortunately, Mr. Thomson didn't hear that, as he was already asleep.

An hour later, he was wakened by the driver once the coach had arrived. The other passengers had already gone, including the two people who had been talking about the mysterious African politician. He took his luggage with him and took a taxi to the hotel.

Mr. Thomson arrived at the reception of the hotel and went through all the checking-in procedure. When everything was finished, the reception girl gave him the key, but then she also suddenly asked him:

"Sir, have you heard about the African politician in Budapest?"

"What?" Mr. Thomson replied, "I have been hearing people talking about it since this morning, but I still have no idea what it is about! Can you tell me what happened?"

"Well, it is a very long story, but the Internet room is just on the second floor, and it is a free service. I am sure it will give you more information."

"I don't need the Internet room. The hotel has a free wireless connection, doesn't it?"

"Yes, the password is on the card key of your room."

Finally, when Mr. Thomson entered his room, the first thing he did was to take out his tablet computer from his luggage, connect to the Internet and look into the mysterious man that he had been hearing about. As soon as he saw the headline on the BBC homepage, he exclaimed, "Oh my God! It's him!"

Who exactly was that politician whom they were all talking about?

Great Parents, Great Son

Do you find that, after reading the story, you find yourself awaiting the identity of the politician? Why are you suddenly interested in a fictitious character who has nothing to do with your real life? The answer is simple: I let you know that there is something interesting, but I don't tell you what exactly it is.

Curiosity is the best way to capture the attention of your readers, as researchers find that the human brain is most sensitive to the perception of novel information in the environment. Therefore, in order to sustain attention, you need to make your readers curious. If, after the first sentence, you can make them wonder: "Why did he say that?" Or: "Why does that happen?", then you have succeeded in buying their time and enticing them to listen to you.

A very good application of this idea comes from a television advertisement for an insurance company. At the beginning of the video, a grown-up tennis player walks into the court, and finds that his opponent is only a kid. Thinking that the kid is only a beginner, the man simply pops the ball to the other side at a very slow speed, so that it is possible for the kid to hit it.

Yet, to the great surprise of the man, the kid hits a very powerful backhander, and sends a winner right to the corner.

Completely stunned, the man tries to play a bit harder. However, he gets beaten by the kid again.

Most audiences will wonder at this point: "Wow, who's that kid?"

The man is not satisfied, so he brings up his best game. The two players exchange some powerful ground strokes. They chase the ball from one corner to another. They move from the baseline to the net, and then back to the baseline again.

Finally, after a hard-fought battle, the man finally won the point. At this moment, the parents of the kid arrive in a car to take him home. It is revealed that the parents of that kid are actually Andre Agassi and Steffi Graff, two great tennis players who are indeed married to each other.

At this point, a narrator delivers the message: the right heritage makes all the difference; we are owned by the largest conglomerate in the country; let's create our legacy together.

There are two outstanding things about this advertisement. Firstly, it pinpoints the most prominent feature of the company (being owned by a famous business group), and repackages it in a graphical way (a great son from great parents,) so that everyone can get the idea immediately. Of course, whether you are owned by a large company has logically nothing to do with whether your products are good. Nevertheless, since it is presented in an easy-to-understand way, people will find it much easier to accept the idea.

Secondly, and more importantly, the advertisement begins in a way that it hooks you up right from the start. Normally, a grown-up beats a kid easily in tennis. However, in the video, you see a kid who is extremely strong and plays better than the man. When you watch it, you cannot help but think, "Why is he so strong? What will the man do?" It immediately generates a lot of questions in your mind, and forces you to go on watching to find the answer.

(As a side note: that boy in the advertisement is not really the son of Agassi and Graff, but just an actor.)

In other words, what the advertisement does can be summarised into two things:

1 It creates an "impossible event" in the beginning, which forces you to watch on to see why.

2 It relates the "impossible event" to a major advantage of the company or the product, which can usually leave a very strong impression on the audience.

Although it is an example from a television advertisement, you can also apply the same principle in a face-to-face sales process, so that you can attract the attention of your prospects immediately. To understand how to do it, let us consider the following paragraph.

The Lure of the Impossible

What is the best way to find more clients and do more business? The answer is actually very simple. In order to make your customers like you, you have to be rude to them. Also, if you price your products higher, it will create more demand. In addition, your company will be more welcomed by your customers if you make more mistakes.

What's your first reaction after reading the above? Most people will think, "What on earth are you talking about? Shouldn't you be nice to your customers, sell at a cheaper price and avoid mistakes?" Yes, of course, but at least, I have got your attention.

The most effective and efficient way to capture people's attention is to begin by something that is obviously wrong. Imagine you have to meet with two insurance agents separately, who are both trying to convince you to buy an insurance policy. The first agent tells you:

"Life insurance is very useful. It can replace your income if you die before your dependents, so that your children can attend university and your family can enjoy a comfortable life."

The second agent tells you:

"Life insurance is not very useful. Even if you have it, you may not get any indemnity after you die, so that your children and family may still suffer as if they had no insurance at all."

Which opener gets you attention more effectively? Of course it is the second one! While almost every insurance agent tells you that it is good to buy insurance, the second agent does the complete opposite. When you hear what he says, you cannot help but think: "Why does he say that? Isn't insurance supposed to protect me?" It stimulates your curiosity, and compels you to wait for the answer.

The reason that it works so well is because our brains do not like illogical things. When we see something that does not look right, our brain will tell us, "Wait, something is wrong! Watch out!" We already exhibit this behaviour as early as in infancy. Developmental psychologists have discovered that when babies see "impossible physical events", such as when an object floats in mid-air, they stare at it for a longer time than usual. This suggests that even infants are attracted to things that are unusual and illogical.

While the above examples may sound a little bit too cheeky for formal situations, you can adjust it to suit your own needs. In an earlier example of a job interview, there is a self-introduction like this:

"I have just graduated from the University of Cambridge in Economics, where I got first-class honours. During my second year, I was the president of the Business School Club, where we held many events for business leaders of tomorrow. Besides that, I also worked as an intern in the Royal Bank of Scotland to familiarise myself with the internal operation of a bank."

Now if it is change to something like this:

"I have just graduated from the University of Cambridge in Economics, where I had the chance to be tutored by a former Nobel Prize winner. During my second year, I was the president of the Business School Club, where I once delivered a speech in front of a member of the Royal Family. Besides that, I also worked as an intern in the Royal Bank of Scotland, where I had the privilege of training other employees, despite the fact that I was only an intern."

It is immediately more interesting. After reading the second version, you immediately want to know:

• Which Nobel Prize winner did he study with?

• How did he give a speech to someone from the Royal Family?

• Why could he train other employees as a mere intern?

And the interviewer will be more interested in asking more about you. So you see, just by putting a little more effort into making your readers curious, you can immediately stand out a lot.

However, there is one problem with using this method: after you throw out the "impossible situation", how can you reconcile the paradox, and relate it to your products or services? If you cannot make a logical continuation from the "impossible situation", you will just look downright stupid. To avoid this problem, let us consider another example.

It's Hard to Become Fat

In the health and fitness market, every single salesperson tells you that slim is good and you must keep fit. They say it because the companies want to sell things such as supplements, gym memberships, beauty treatments and so on. Suppose you are a fitness coach, how will you approach your customers so that you can catch their attention immediately?

Applying the logic of "impossible situations", one way to begin the process is by telling your prospects:

"Please do not keep fit! Go eat as much as you like! Never do any exercise!"

Surely, the first reaction of your listeners will be, "Why?"

Then he tells you, "Because it is easy to lose weight, but hard to get fat!"

"What? Isn't it instead easy to get fat, and hard to become fit?" many people may ask.

After stunning them with two unusual statements, you can begin to explain:

"These are two photos of my customer, May. This was her six months ago. As you can see, she was quite fat, and she remained like that for six years." Then you show them another picture of a slim woman:

"However, after joining my programme, she is now slim and hot. So, if it takes six years to get fat, but just six months to get fit, isn't it fair to say the latter is easier?"

This is a very successful application of what you have just read about. Firstly, you behave in a completely different way from the rest of the salespeople. While everyone tells them to get fit, you tell them to get fat. After that, you stun them further with an illogical statement: it is hard to get fat but easy to keep fit. It immediately arouses the curiosity of your listeners, and makes them want to know more.

Yet the latter part is even more brilliant. You employed a false logic to justify your earlier illogical statement. You mentioned a testimonial of an existing client who took a very short time to get into shape after being fat for many years, so it must be very easy to get slim. The good thing is, by the way, that you also indirectly suggest to your prospects that if they become your clients, they can get slim in a short time too.

The reason that you can make such a smooth transition from your opening to your service is that you used a pseudo-logic called generalisation. Here is an example:

- Winston Churchill is bald.

- My father is bald.

- Winston Churchill is my father.

The above is obviously wrong, because while my father is bald, not everyone who is bald is my father. In other words, "being bald" is one of the features of "my father", so that it alone cannot qualify anyone to become the latter.

This is also the trick used in the above fitness coach example. While an easy task usually takes a short time to finish, it does not mean that something is easy just because it is done in a short time. However, it is enough for you to justify the earlier paradox, and start talking about your fitness class.

Don't Save Money

Here is one more example. Suppose you are a financial adviser who wants to persuade your clients to invest their savings. Using the method of "impossible situations", when you meet a client, you can begin by telling him:

"You should not save money. Instead, you should spend money as often as possible! This is because it is hard to spend money, but easy to earn money."

And when the client asks you why, you can tell him:

"I have a client called Tom who started a saving plan with me five years ago. When he began, he always saved a tenth of his income, and spent half of it every month. Now the value of his total investment has already tripled in value. Isn't it easy to earn money if you can triple your money by spending five times more than you save?"

Again, it is a false logic, but with that you successfully point out that saving money is easy and affordable. It generates the interest of your clients to start saving immediately.

However, this is not the only way to play with this opening. As well as speaking about how easy it is to get rich, you can also do it in the opposite way. If I see an older client who is going to retire soon, I will begin with the same opening paragraph (i.e. "hard to spend money, but easy to earn money"), yet I will use a different interpretation. When they ask me why I say that, I will explain:

"Out of ten clients I see every day, nine of them do not think about their finances. This is why I tell you it is easy to spend money, but hard to save, because everyone does the former instead of the latter. Yet this is very unfortunate, because when they reach retirement age, they will usually be forced to keep on working, instead of retiring comfortably."

The two versions target completely different clienteles. While the first one sells hope (i.e. easy to earn money), the second one sells fear (i.e. penniless retirement). Deciding which one to use is completely dependent on whom you are selling to. If your client is a young fellow, then it is more logical to use the first one, because retirement is too far away for him. On the other hand, the second one will appeal more to older people, because they are near retirement and they have a genuine fear about that.

As well as that, it also depends on what you are selling. If you are selling a fund with aggressive returns, then it obviously makes more sense to sell hope. However, if you are selling something like medical insurance, then the second version will be more suitable for you.

In summary, it is safe to conclude that you will have a much better chance in prospecting if you can arouse the curiosity of your listeners. However, even though the idea of "impossible situation" is very powerful, it only solves half of the problems you face in approaching your prospects.

Getting into the topic

Approaching prospects can be done under two kinds of situations. The first one is a formal approach, and common methods include cold calling and door-to-door visits. When the customer is approached this way, you can talk freely about business from the first minute because the customer already knows that you are going to talk about it, and wants you to come to the point as soon as possible.

However, sometimes you may also meet your potential customers in an informal situation, such as at your friend's birthday party, or an amateur sports team where you are one of the players. Under this kind of situation, you cannot get serious immediately and talk about business, because you will immediately be labelled as yet another annoying salesman, and it will make it harder to build rapport with your targets.

Usually, there are two kinds of approaches in this situation. The first kind of person is the do-or-die type. They bring up the business topic anyway, and try to convince other people to do business with them. Although it is very efficient, in the long term it will simply damage their relationships with the people they know. The second kind is more conservative, and they try to avoid business and start with small talk first. Although it can avoid looking too aggressive, they often suffer from a low conversion rate.

So, you can neither be too aggressive nor too conservative. What should you do instead?

5. Covert Advertising

A Failure in Online Marketing

Thanks to the efforts of Scarlett, the Mr. Thomson's business was slowly becoming more and more profitable. Mr. Thomson thought that it would be a great idea to further promote the shop and let more people know about it, so he became an online marketer himself and wrote about his shop everywhere on the Internet.

Every night, Mr. Thomson would go to different forums and websites and leave a comment or two in each of them. Here are some examples:

• I've just found a new shop called Kyle's Boutique. The clothes are very nice. I always go there to find new clothes.

• My girlfriend bought me a very nice jacket. I asked her where she bought it. She said it was from a new shop called Kyle's Boutique.

- I bought a nice shirt from a place called Kyle's Boutique, but I don't need it anymore. I think I'd like to sell it.

Unfortunately, the response was at best lukewarm even after a few weeks. Mr. Thomson thought perhaps he should write more aggressively to attract more attention, so he posted more frequently and aggressively in different forums by using different accounts to post similar things.

Unfortunately, it backfired. The forum members started to smell what he was doing. One member replied and said:

"You seem to be very keen on the shop you are talking about."

"Damn, perhaps I've overdone it," thought Mr. Thomson, and he replied, "No, I just mentioned it because I happened to come across it, and I think it is quite good."

However, he had no idea that the member would then shoot back:

"In that case, I am very interested to see that you are posting the same message in several other forums as well." Then the member posted several hypertext links, all of which linked to other pages where Mr. Thomson had copy-and-pasted the same paragraphs.

"Oh no," thought Mr. Thomson, and in order to avoid further trouble, he decided to delete the post immediately.

Unfortunately, it was too late. The moderator of the forum had already noticed it, and gave Mr. Thomson a warning that if he posted something like that again he would be banned.

Discouraged by his failure, Mr. Thomson told this story to Scarlett, and she laughed.

"Oh come on," said Mr. Thomson, "Being embarrassed like that isn't very funny. You'd know if you were in my position."

"I understand that," said Scarlett, "but it strikes me that it is hard to prevent such embarrassment when you are so obvious in promoting yourself."

"But how can you be not obvious when you are doing marketing?"

"I think your messages should be put in a more subtle way," said Scarlett. "How about this: I will write you several passages to post on different forums, and in return you will give me a fiver for each of them?"

"Sounds like a plan," said Mr. Thomson. "But of course I'll have to review the things you write before I decide whether I want to pay or not."

"Well, most certainly," said Scarlett.

If you were Scarlett, how would you help Mr. Thomson?

What Is Deliberate Is Cheap

Imagine one day you suddenly discover a very good business, which allows you to generate at least 100 per cent of return every year, and you also have enough time and capital to put it into action. Will you go everywhere and tell everyone about this very good business idea of yours?

Of course you will not! Instead, you will keep it as much a secret as possible. You will never tell anyone about it – not even some of your closest friends. The reason is very simple: why should I share something so juicy with you when I can take it all myself?

Now let us consider another example. Suppose you are running a business, and it is doing fairly well. However, you know that there will be a major technological change, which will hurt your business forever. Now, only you and a few insiders know about this upcoming change, and the public do not know about it yet. What will you do in this situation?

Obviously, you will do the complete opposite of what you would do in the first example. You will go everywhere and tell everyone:

"I have a very good business. It has been earning money every year, and I am really very proud of it. In the past, some large companies have tried to take it over, but I refused. However, now I am thinking about retirement, and I want to spend more time with my family. So, I will consider selling it if you can offer me a good price."

But of course, most people are not stupid, and they understand human nature as well. When they see you keeping on telling them that you have something good, they know there are only two possibilities:

1. You have an extreme sense of vanity, so that you are hungry for approval from others.

2. You are just desperate to sell your business to someone else, and possibly not for a good reason.

With this logic, it is not hard to understand why it is a very bad idea to be too obvious and aggressive when you try to sell anything. The more aggressively you sell, the more desperate you look; and the more desperate you look, the more people will doubt your motives. In other words, you appear to need them more than they need you.

In fact, the most famous and competitive sellers are usually the least desperate in promoting themselves. For example, when you look at the credit card market, it is usually the smaller providers that offer you the best discounts and rebates, because they are not well known and they have to offer more to attract customers. On the other hand, the big banks already have plenty of existing customers, and most people have confidence in them, so their offers are usually less attractive.

In summary, the more desperately you tell people that something is good, the more they will doubt you. Therefore, when you try to promote yourself, you should always try to avoid looking desperate. Unfortunately, this is a mistake made by many junior salespeople, especially a particular kind of vendors: the multilevel marketers.

The Most Effective Way to Lose Friends

For those who have no idea, multilevel marketing (or MLM in short) is one of the most effective, but yet also notorious ways of marketing. The commission structure means that the sales force are compensated not only by their own sales, but also those by the other salespeople that they recruit – otherwise known as the "down-lines."

Therefore, people in MLM can generate passive income in two forms:

1 When their down-lines make sales.

2 When new members pay a fee to become their down-lines.

Under this structure, people in MLM usually try to recruit as many people as possible, so that everyone starting out in MLM is encouraged to recruit their friends and family. Unfortunately, since their approach to recruiting members is usually quite hard-selling, it usually affects the relationships between the MLM people and the friends whom they try to recruit.

A long time ago, I got to know a girl called Louise for a few months. One day, out of the blue, she invited me to have lunch on a forthcoming Sunday. Since I had nothing to do that day, I agreed to go. However, on the day, I encountered something very strange.

We started our conversation by talking about our backgrounds. Louise told me that she worked in a cosmetic company. Although she tried not to look as though she was bragging, she was clearly attempting to let me know about the expensive car that she had, and the expensive flat she had just bought in London. She went on and on about how great her life was.

Although her self-glorification was a bit too much, I still congratulated her on being so successful. Unfortunately, I had no idea that it would only encourage Louise to continue.

She then told me that she was from a poor family, and had worked in several horrible jobs after graduating. She did not lack the adjectives to describe the unfortunate days during which she had worked long hours for low pay. After babbling about how hideous her life had been, however, she suddenly started to describe how grateful she was to have joined the current company, and how successful she had been ever since.

I had already smelled something wrong, and was beginning to realise why I had been invited there in the first place. To confirm my suspicion, I went straight to the point:

"That sounds like a very interesting business. Would you mind telling me which company you are working for?"

Oddly enough, instead of revealing the name of the company right away, Louise went on to describe the background of the company, and explain how great it was, and how many young people had become very successful after joining it. I was getting a bit frustrated, so I pressed on:

"That sounds excellent. However, I have been with a similar company before. Would you mind letting me know the name of it?"

Finally, Louise told me the name of the company. It was a big multi-level marketing company incorporated in America, and sold personal care products and dietary supplements. Having finally got the name, I added:

"Oh! I have already joined that company under my aunt, but I am sure we can find a lot of opportunities to cooperate in future." I gave her a polite but firm reason to reject her attempt to recruit me.

Seeing that all the doors were shut, Louise also decided to bring it to an end: "I see, since you are such an excellent personality, your aunt must be very happy for having you."

Obviously, the sole purpose of suddenly inviting a stranger like me for lunch was to recruit me into her team. Unfortunately, her selling techniques were just too horrible to convince anybody. However, that was not the end of it.

Many months later, I bumped into Louise again. I greeted her, but her reaction was very cold. Later, I learned that she had already given up MLM and gone back to her old job. Being an MLM must have been a painful experience for her, but it was hardly surprising to me. She was just too direct and aggressive when she was trying to sell things to people – yet as the following example would show, persuasion is most effectively done with subtlety and indirectness.

The Power of Referral

Several years ago, a Premier League football club in England was trying to convince the fans to sign up for its text bulletin service. Basically, the idea is that, for 25p a message, fans would get a text whenever something interesting happened at the club, such as team selections, injury updates, half-time scores and so on.

Sadly, despite the promotion efforts of the club, the results were not very encouraging. They had tried traditional methods such as advertising the service in club literature and on the club website, and sending out hordes of young women to hand out leaflets on match days. Nevertheless, the club could not get more than a lowly 20 subscriptions a week, so it decided to try a more innovative approach.

They hired a small marketing agency, which specialised in a new form of marketing called stealth marketing. In essence, they got a group of 15 actors, who all pretended to be fans of the football club, and visited different pubs and bars on the match days. Each time, there would be two to three people in a group, and they visited each pub for about half an hour.

And what did they do during their visit of each pub? They basically just chatted with the fans there. However, at a certain point in the conversation, the actors would pull something out of their pockets. It turned out to be some crumpled-up leaflet. When the innocent football fans asked them what it was, they would tell them that it was a text bulletin service of the club. After that, they would show them their own mobile phones, and demonstrate how it worked. They repeated this process in pub after pub to talk to different fans.

And what was the result? It was mentioned that the club had been getting hardly more than 20 subscriptions every week before this. After the first week of stealth marketing, the club had a whopping 120 new sign-ups for that week! But that was not the end of it. In the second week, it increased to 125. In the third week, they got 75, and 60 the following week.

If you think that this stealth marketing strategy is only applicable to silly little things like football messaging, then you may have got a terribly wrong idea. The same company that promoted the above text bulletin service had worked for many other bigger clients as well. For example, they had hired actors to dress like ordinary citizens, and, in front of other people, express some very positive comments about a major UK newspaper that they were reading.

The company had even approached a mainstream political party in the UK before an election, and suggested that they pay for teams of stooges to wander around marginal constituencies and sing the praises of their manifesto. However, the party declined for fear of catastrophic exposure, but they agreed that it was a very clever idea.

Why was this method so effective? The reason is very simple. If an ordinary salesman approaches you and tells you about a product he sells, you will immediately activate your "mental firewall" and think, "Damn, another bloody salesman." However, if an innocent person approaches you and mentions the product during the chat, you will think, "Oh, it must be a great one if he recommends that. I will try it one day."

This is the power of third-party referral. As stated in the first chapter, it is not about what you say, or even how you say it, but about who you are. If you are a salesman, you are immediately perceived as a biased person whose sole objective is to sell things. It has nothing to do with you as a person, but your credibility has instantly diminished. Whatever you tell people will be more cautiously taken and conservatively considered.

This is why traditional advertisements are dying. In 2004, Deutsche Bank conducted a study and found that, in the short term, only 18 per cent of television campaigns in the US actually generated a positive return on investment. In the long term, it is slightly higher, but only as much as 45 per cent. In other words, over half of the advertising effort on the televisions actually loses money.

Of course, there is a good way and a bad way of doing anything. Even though stealth marketing is effective, it is only the case if it is done right. In the story at the beginning, Mr. Thomson also tried to pretend to be a third party recommending his own business. However, it did not generate a lot of interest because his work was too obvious and uninteresting. So how should he have done it instead? Let us return to the story.

The Trojan of Communication

After a few days, Scarlett composed a few stories for Mr. Thomson to post on different forums. Here is one example which was to be posted on a local business forum:

"Last week, I flew to China for a business trip, and I found that your dress code is really important for doing business with the Chinese. A veteran told me that the Chinese like us a lot if we show that we like their culture. For women like us, it is better to wear something related to their tradition.

"However, when you dress in a Chinese costume, there are two things to which you should pay attention. Firstly, the Chinese have a completely different perception of colours from Westerners. While we wear white for happy events and black for sad ones, the Chinese do the total opposite: they wear black (and red) when they are happy.

"Secondly, you should avoid anything with too many glaring dragons, tigers or any 'Chinese' patterns on it, because they are nothing more than exaggerated costumes, which are only seen in Western films. Most Chinese people do not wear those. Instead, the Chinese culture values subtlety, so simplicity and elegance are highly appreciated.

"Unfortunately, it is hard to find Chinese clothes that fulfil the above requirements, because, well, the 'Chinese' things we have here are too 'westernised'. I searched many places, but still could not find any.

"Then I was totally surprised to find a very beautiful Chinese dress in a small shop called the Kyle's Boutique near the train station. It is very similar to the one worn by the leading actress in *Lust, Caution* (directed by Ang Lee). It is very good-looking, but elegant enough to be not too glaring. It is quite amazing that although the shop was quite small, I was able to find such a beautiful dress there.

"So I learnt that when you look for clothes that are not of the mainstream, you should always try the small ones, like the one I just visited. They may have some pleasant surprises for you."

When you read the above story, you do not feel that it is hard-selling anything to you at all. Quite the contrary, you feel that you have learned something new and interesting. Despite that, you still somehow receive the message that the boutique mentioned is a good one. It is therefore quite a successful piece of advertising.

The reason that it works so well is that it is able to sugar-coat the true message within an interesting lecture on Chinese costumes. Your conscious attention is somehow decoyed by the wonderful story, so that it allows the good image of the boutique to silently creep into your subconscious mind. In other words, the Chinese costumes information acts as a "Trojan Horse" to carry the hidden message across the critical barrier of the readers' minds.

For those who are not very familiar with history, the Trojan horse is a tale from an ancient war between the Greeks and the Trojans. After a fruitless 10-year siege of the city of Troy, the Greeks thought of a subterfuge that allowed them to enter the city and end the conflict. They presented a huge wooden horse in front of the city then sailed away. Thinking that it was a token of victory, the Trojans pulled the horse inside the city, and celebrated their war effort.

However, there was actually a team of Greek soldiers hidden inside the horse. Under the cover of night, they sneaked out of the horse and opened the city gate, where the army, which had pretended to sail away, had already returned. They entered the city and defeated the Trojans.

Therefore, if you also want to make a successful advertisement like the above, you should include the following three elements, which could be summarised as the Three S's:

1 The Setup: an unrelated story to cover the true message. In this case, it is the adventure to find a suitable dress for the China trip.

2 The Suggestion: the true message to be broadcasted. In this case, it is the positive image of the boutique.

3 The Seminar: some interesting lesson which can surely capture the attention of the readers. In this case, it is how to choose a good Chinese dress.

The third point, Seminar, is very important. Everyone likes to learn something, especially when it is novel and useful. In this example, the passage was posted on an online business forum, and many businessmen have to do business with China. The idea that they can learn something about the Chinese is a huge attraction to them. It creates the incentive for them to read the story, or even share it on other forums.

(Note: all information regarding the Chinese costume in the above story is true.)

Whenever you approach people you have never met before at a social event such as a cocktail party, you can also use this technique to let them know about your business.

Approaching in Social Situations

As stated at the end of the last chapter, there are two kinds of approaching: formal and social. In a formal meeting, you can come to the point and start selling quickly, as the customer fully expects that. However, in social situations, people don't want to talk about business when they want to have fun, so you must sell yourself to them indirectly.

Suppose you run an I.T. company that provides services to small and medium enterprises. One day, when you go to a cocktail party, you meet the owner of a start-up retailer business, who might be your potential customer. How can you covertly sell your company without it looking deliberate? You can start by telling him:

"I have a client who runs a shop of her own, where she sells ladies' items such as handbags designed by her. One day, she told me that she would like to expand her business online so she can sell her things directly through the Internet. However, after listening to the details of her plan I was a bit worried."

"Why were you worried?" The listener may ask you.

"Well, she said she would like to process payments through a third-party entity called PayGal. She said it is the most popular online payment platform nowadays, and many people are using that. Many people would find it convenient to buy things from her through PayGal. However..."

"What's wrong with PayGal?"

"The point is, even though PayGal is really convenient, there are actually some fatal pitfalls for the seller!"

"Really?"

"Yes. One of their most harmful policies is their questionable 'dispute resolution centre', which allows the buyer to file a complaint to the seller. To be fair, it also covers the seller in event of an unauthorised purchase, an 'item not received' claim, chargeback or reversal. However, shrewd buyers could simply come up with an alternative excuse, such as 'item not as described', and refuse to pay."

"But can't they trace the buyers through the number and the address?"

"Not always. In other countries such as the US, there is a General Delivery method, where the person can collect the parcel with his name only, without the exact address. The number, of course, could also be a fake one.

"To make it worse, when you sell things through PayGal, you have to agree to accept that the resolution decision of the issuing bank is final and legally binding, but for most of the time the issuing banks are in favour of their customers. So I suggested my to client that she use a better method."

"What's the better method?"

"To develop her company's payment platform through us. Of course, it is not easy to manage it, but our company has already worked with several large companies for their secure payment channels, and we have a first-rate data encryption technology. So far, she was happy with our service, and it is working well for her."

The above story is about a business owner who wants to develop an online selling platform. To make it more appealing, it also teaches you how to avoid a "secret pitfall" when working with a third-party payment platform. But of course, the true intention of the story is to tell you that the speaker's company provides a very good service for setting up online business. (Note: again, all information regarding the potential dangers of a third-party platform is true.)

Preparing Your Story

Obviously, you have to prepare for stories like this beforehand. Roughly speaking, there are two kinds of topics you can talk about: business-related and business-unrelated. Of course, it would be most direct if you were to start with a topic related to your business. The advantage is that you can quickly relate your value to your listeners. The above story is exactly this case. Even though he did not directly sell his company, it indirectly shows that if you can become his customer he will provide you a very excellent service.

However, it is impossible to use business as a topic if your products or services are not directly related to the listener's job. Suppose you are an insurance agent, it is not easy to tell a story about your clients in a social situation, because then people may suspect that you are trying to sell insurance to them. Therefore, you have to talk about something else.

In this case, you have to talk about things that are only remotely related to your business. Suppose you are having a chat with someone about your university life, you can tell them a story like this to sell insurance indirectly:

"You know, even though I am an insurance agent, I used to study physics in a university. I once knew a very eccentric Professor Johnson, who was one of the most robotic persons I have ever met. He walked very slowly and awkwardly, and always spoke in a mechanical word-by-word manner, so that it always took him an hour to finish his sentence. One day, however, he mutated into another person.

"At the end of the term, my friends and I went to a restaurant where there was a public karaoke stage. At one point, I saw someone I knew go on to the stage, ready to sing. Do you know who he was? Yes, it was Professor Johnson! At first I thought it would be a comic performance by a robotic professor, but I was wrong! He was singing the disco song *Moves like Jagger* by Maroon 5, and we were totally surprised! Few would expect a boring-looking professor like him to be able to sing so well. We all applauded after he had finished, and I went to the stage to find him.

"I asked him how come he could sing so well. He told me that he was from a poor family. When he was young, his father died. Unfortunately, he did not have any insurance to claim an indemnity, so his son was forced to work at the same time as studying. However, it was a lot of pressure for him to perform well at school while working part-time, so he had to find some ways to let go of his stress.

"That was how he came to sing. At first he just sang inside his room, but he soon found that it was a nuisance for his family, so he started to go to a karaoke place. Slowly, it became his hobby and he became very good at it. I used to think that karaoke was just a silly entertainment, but my opinion changed completely after this event."

Of course, the true message of the above story is that you will leave a horrible burden on your family if you die without any insurance. However, it is a perfectly reasonable story to be told in a social situation, because it is an interesting story itself, and on the surface you are just talking about your professor.

This is why the skill of storytelling is essential in the arsenal of a good salesman, because you can bring your message across to your listeners without looking as though you are hard-selling. Nevertheless, there is one more dimension you can add to your story if you want to make it even more effective.

The "Impossible" Character

Unless you are working in a monopoly business, there are usually many competitors in your field. If a customer does not buy from you, he will still have the chance to buy from someone else. Therefore, it is essential for you to make a strong impression on your prospects, so that the next time they need your products they will remember you first instead of your competitors.

One of the best ways to make people remember you is to make them curious about you. As explained in the last chapter, curiosity is the best way to get the attention of others. While the last chapter focuses on creating curiosity about your products, here you will learn how to make people curious about you yourself.

Let us refer back to the Professor Johnson story above. At the beginning of the story, he appeared to be dull and boring. However, later, it was revealed that he had a karaoke hobby, and was very good at it. It leaves a strong impression on the listeners, because the two images ("robotic professor" and "great pop singer") are totally incompatible. It creates an "impossible character" and, as explained in the last chapter, people have the strongest memory for "impossible" things.

You can apply the same idea to yourself. Suppose you are a financial adviser, whose image is very commercial and practical, you can talk about your interest in arts and philosophy. Or if you are a salesgirl of beauty products, you can tell people about your masculine interests such as kick-boxing – which is out-of-character with your beautiful image. It will make people think, "Wow, I can't believe that this beautiful chick is actually a fighter."

Better yet, you should combine your "impossible habit" with the storytelling strategy described earlier in the chapter, so that you will not only sell your products, but also you yourself. Here is a short example. Suppose you are a programmer who looks very much like a computer geek, you can tell people a story like this:

"As you know, most programmers are computer geeks, and I used to be one of them. One day, a friend told me that I should learn something less geeky, otherwise I wouldn't be able to find a girlfriend. So he introduced me to Salsa dancing.

"When I started, I began with the basic moves. Since I am a very bright student, I remembered all the moves very soon. I felt like I had already got the idea, and was ready to dance with someone else. However, when I started to dance with a girl, I suddenly had no idea how to move, because I was not in sync with the music.

"It was only later when I met a good teacher who taught me to appreciate the rhythm of dancing that I realised that dancing is not just mechanically moving in a specific way, but becoming one with the music, and moving in sync with the beat. If you have to choose between knowing all the moves and learning how to dance with the music, then you should choose the latter without thinking.

"Having understood that, as a programmer, I wrote a mobile phone app to help beginners to learn Salsa several months ago, and it emphasises helping the user to understand the rhythm of the music. To my surprise, it was selected by the Mobile Premier Awards as one of the winners last year."

(Note: again, all information regarding Salsa dancing in the story is true.)

The above short story achieves two things: firstly, it pairs up a "geeky" programmer with Salsa dancing, and creates an interesting contrast. Secondly, it also points out that he was an award-winning programmer.

Of course, you may not have a hobby that is in such sharp contrast to your image, but such a habit may be worth investing in. You do not have to know a lot about the hobby. You just need to know enough to make up stories to assist your prospecting in social events. In the age of the Internet, a little research with Google and Wikipedia can already provide enough background for you.

The information of these two chapters should be enough to help you to approach your targets with minimal resistance, and arouse their interest in the shortest time possible. Now here is the next question: how to turn an initial interest into a true desire to buy?

Needs vs. Wants

Many consultants and salespeople believe that it is good professional practice to discover and address the needs of their clients before making any recommendations. They usually follow a three-step approach like this:

1 Understand the background of the client.

2 Establish goals based on their situation.

3 Suggests products/services to achieve the goals.

For example, when a financial adviser sees a client, he first wants to know how old he is, how much he earns and what investments he has. Secondly, he estimates how much the client will need when he retires, or to achieve a specific goal he might have in life. Finally, he outlines a plan of how much the client should invest in order to meet the needs.

Surely, this is a very sound principle of consulting? However, the consultants who follow this approach usually encounter a problem. They may not have any difficulty in getting their clients to talk or in understanding their needs, yet when they present their proposals to their clients, they do not always seem very interested. Instead, they usually just say they have to "think about it" before making any decision, and then disappear without a trace. Why do they fail to convince their clients even though they have addressed their needs?

The reason is very simple: people buy what they want, not what they need.

A need is something that is objectively essential for surviving. For instance, we all have to eat. If I am very hungry, then no matter how hard it is to find food, I still need to find something to eat, otherwise I will die. On the other hand, if I am already full, no matter how delicious the food is, I am not going to eat anything.

In real life, people more often buy what they want than what they need. For example, when a lady buys some new clothes, it is not because her old clothes are no longer wearable, but because the new clothes look good to her, even though she does not need them at all. Her desire to look good in her new clothes is a stronger influence than her actual need.

Similarly, when a teenager begins to smoke, it is not because he needs nicotine to survive, but because he thinks smoking looks cool. In other words, it is his desire to look cool that makes him smoke, even though he knows logically that smoking is harmful to his health.

Therefore, in any kind of persuasion, it is the desire instead of the need that you have to work on. However, human desires are very illusive, so how can you take advantage of them? To answer this question, let us look at the next chapter.

6. Rapid Rapport

If You're a Gentleman

Joe was the most terrible kid you could ever imagine. At the age of 12, he was expelled from school for misdemeanours such as violence and vandalism. At the same time, he stabbed animals on his father's farm with a pitchfork and set fire to the barn. His parents decided that they had had enough, so they took their son to court and committed him to the House of Refuge for Juvenile Delinquents.

At 15, Joe was paroled by the House, but he was soon arrested for burglary on his way home, so that he had to stay at the House again until he was 21. By the time he was released again, both his parents were dead. Unfortunately, they had already determined to leave nothing for Joe, and donated everything to charity in to their will.

However, he did not need the money anyway, as he was soon caught again for burglary and assault, and was sentenced to a more serious term in the state prison. After serving every day of that term, he was released and headed back home again. As soon as he walked into the town, everybody started screaming, "Look out! Joe's back!"

Sure enough, a week after he had arrived back in town, shopkeepers reported items missing from their shops, and householders also discovered that their belongings had suddenly started to disappear – including an expensive motorboat. Everybody knew who the culprit was.

At the same time, it turned out that there was a rich farmer who lived just outside the town. He had a daughter named Susie, who was the most attractive lady in the area. However, even though she was extremely popular among the young men, no one could understand why she was still single and had no boyfriend.

One day, when Susie was walking down the street, Joe just happened to be leaning up against a wall on the side. When he saw Susie coming, Joe swung around and stood in her path. He looked her up and down very thoroughly and very quietly, and Susie, with equal poise, looked Joe up and down very thoroughly too.

Finally, Joe said, "Can I take you dancing this Friday?"

Susie said, "You can if you're a gentleman."

And Joe just stepped out of the way and let Susie go.

Strangely enough, the next morning the shopkeepers who had reported missing items found boxes full of stolen goods back at their front doors, and the missing motorboat was suddenly back where it belonged. And that Friday, everybody was surprised to see Joe and Susie go dancing together. And they danced every dance – just the two of them.

Soon after that, people discovered that Joe had started working in Susie's family farm, and he turned out to be one of the best workers they had ever hired. In addition to dancing on Friday, Joe and Susie also began to go to Church together. Within a year, they married.

Joe soon became one of the most popular people in the town. His old days were soon forgotten about, and he was even elected to be the president of the local school board. Later, Joe would even start his own rehabilitation programme by volunteering in the state reformatory, and brought back a few young men from there to work on his farm.

And the story concluded, "All the psychotherapy that Joe required was: 'You can if you're a gentleman.'"

Who Am I?

The above is actually one of the teaching tales of the famous psychotherapist Milton Erickson. Although it seems quite amazing that Joe could be transformed into a model citizen just by a simple sentence, it is not impossible. According to the study of psychology, the decision-making of a man can be roughly divided into two parts:

- Identity: What role am I assuming?

- Behaviour: What should I do under this situation?

Here is a very simple example. John is a very talkative and enthusiastic person, and laughs a lot when he is with his friends. However, when he is at work he suddenly becomes very cold and reserved because his office has a very serious working atmosphere, and his boss does not like people to talk too much. John's personality is still the same, but placing him in a different role changes his behaviour.

Therefore, one of the best ways to change a person is to change his role or position, so that he will modify his behaviour to accommodate. As an example, we can look at one of the most famous people in European history – Napoleon Bonaparte.

Napoleon was born on a small island called Corsica, which was ruled by the French government. When he was young, he was in favour of Corsican independence from France. He once wrote: "On Corsica I was given life, and with that life I was also given a fierce love for this my ill-starred homeland and fierce desire for her independence. I too shall one day be a 'Paoli.'" He was referring to General Pasquale Paoli, who was the embodiment of Corsican resistance, and was passionately worshipped by the young Napoleon.

However, after he became the Emperor of France, he adopted a very different perspective. He had completely forgotten about his young dream of Corsican Independence. And not only did he have no plans to let Corsica escape from his rule, but he also aggressively annexed many other countries of Europe and turned them into new additions of the French Empire. France, which was once his archenemy, became his most important asset to fulfil his own ambition.

In summary, change the identity and you change the behaviour. However, the change in identity does not always have to occur in terms of social position, as in the above examples. If the self-perceived identity of a person changes, even though there is no change in objective status, his behaviour will change as well. To illustrate the point, here is a little personal experience of mine.

A Polite Way to Shut People up

Working in the financial industry, my job requires me to do seminars on the financial market every now and then. Very often, these seminars are promotional in nature – i.e. the primary purpose of the talks is to make you aware of our company, or better yet, let us manage your money for you, so that we can earn a bit of "maintenance fee" along the way.

Therefore, most of these seminars are usually free of charge. You can attend as long as you sign up for it. Unfortunately, since it is free, people usually do not take it seriously. Sometimes they talk freely on their mobile phones, or even chat with each other. Although it does not happen very often, it is not very comfortable when it does.

One day, when I was doing one of those talks, I was unfortunate enough to find such people in the audience. Honestly, if it had just been a few sentences exchanged, I would not have minded. However, there were two people who talked continuously for a whole minute, and it was beginning to disturb other listeners. So I told them:

"Excuse me, could you please keep it down?"

They apologised and shut up... for a while. Some minutes later, they started to talk again.

This time, someone else reminded them to keep quiet, and they stopped talking.

Unfortunately, after a while, they began a conversation for the third time.

When I saw that, I decided that I should do something. Usually, when speakers see this kind of situation, there are two kinds of response:

1 They just leave it and let them talk.

2 They escalate their warning.

The first strategy is useful if the people who are talking are not very persistent. However, if they have been disturbing people and you do nothing, you will lose the respect of the audience, and they will think: "You are in charge of the situation, yet you decide to remain quiet when you see something that is obviously wrong?" This is very detrimental when you are actually trying to sell your company because it will leave a very bad impression.

On the other hand, however, you cannot get too aggressive, either. Everyone has a certain degree of self-esteem. No one likes to be ordered around or look inferior in front of others. If I just went about shouting at them, "You bastards! Couldn't you just keep quiet?" they might shoot back at me and say, "Hey, you surely don't have to shout like that, do you?" Then it might turn into an argument and disturb everybody.

I understood that if I were just to say something ordinary to ask them to keep quiet, they would soon begin to talk again. So I decided I would have to say something more creative that would have a better effect. So I told them:

"Hi, you two can keep talking, there is no problem with that..."

"What?" Their expression told me that they were completely perplexed, because people usually told them to shut up – not to keep talking. Of course I deliberately said the opposite because, as you learned in the fourth chapter, it created an "impossible situation", which captured their attention immediately. And after I had their attention, I continued:

"I have heard you discussing something for a long time. It must be something important. However, since I am paid by my company here to analyse the market, I must try my best to get it done. When you are talking here, I cannot concentrate on my job. Perhaps you could continue your discussion outside?"

And then they apologised for the third time, but after this time they never talked again.

The reason why it worked so effectively was that it created a dissonance between their identity and behaviour. Let us analyse the above passage:

- First, it said that they "must be talking about something important". While it was obviously not true, it put them under a label that they were good people who did not intend to disturb others.

- On the behaviour level, however, it also pointed out that they were indeed disturbing other people. Therefore, they were not doing something that was consistent with the "good people" label.

It forced them to reconcile the difference between their identity and behaviour. Usually, the identity side wins, because everyone wants to be a good person and look good in front of others, so that they would rather correct their behaviours than to remain being "bad people."

Cognitive Dissonance

In psychology, this phenomenon is called cognitive dissonance, which refers to the discomfort experienced by the subject when he finds a conflict between his belief and his behaviour. Many psychological studies have found it to be one of the most powerful ways to influence people. Here is a little experiment that exactly demonstrates this point.

This experiment was done by two female researchers at a swimming pool. Female swimmers were recruited as they exited the pool area, and were on their way to the locker room. A female researcher, disguised as a member of a water conservation office, approached each potential subject and asked if she could spare a few moments to help with a water conservation project.

If the subject answered yes, the researcher would ask the subjects some questions regarding their water-saving habits, and ask them to sign a flyer to commit to saving water in the future. After that, the subject was thanked and she headed to the changing room.

However, unbeknown to the subjects, there was actually a second researcher waiting in the shower room. She unobtrusively timed the length of each subject's shower, and noted whether subjects turned off the water flow while soaping up.

The result was that those who had answered the questionnaire and signed the flyer would take significantly less time to shower than the control group who were not approached by researchers. In addition, the "committed" people were also more likely to turn off the water flow when they soaped up. The reason for this outcome was that the questionnaire and the flyer reminded the subjects that, although they thought they supported saving water, they were not actually putting it into practice every day. It created a cognitive dissonance and changed their behaviour.

It is similar in Erickson's teaching tale. When Joe invited Susie to dance, her reply was: "You can if you are a gentleman." It communicated two things:

- On the identity level, it meant that Joe was a gentleman who was worthy of a beautiful lady.

- However, on the behaviour level, it also meant that he was not doing what a gentleman was supposed to do.

Facilitated by the fact that he was promised a dance with a beautiful lady, this simple sentence brought about an immediate change in a person whom everyone thought was a lost cause. Again, when the chance came, even a scoundrel like Joe wished to be recognised as a good man after being known to be otherwise for most of his life.

In conclusion, one of the most effective ways to influence others is by following this two-step process:

1 Label them with an image that is consistent with the way you want them to behave.

2 Point out the discrepancy between the image and their behaviour.

It all sounds very simple, doesn't it? Unfortunately, while this concept is very easy to understand, it is not the same when it comes to the application. In fact, when most people try to use this method, they usually make a fatal mistake that makes the whole tactic backfire.

The Invisible Shark

When an insurance agent tries to persuade someone to buy life insurance, he always tells the prospect:

"Mr. Prospect, you are a very responsible man. You want your family to live happily. You do not want your family to lose their comfortable life in case of an accident happening to you. If you want to protect them, you will have to minimise the damage of a potential catastrophe with an insurance policy."

In the above example, the agent tries to label the prospect as someone who is supposed to protect his family, so he ought to buy insurance from him. However, if you are the prospect you will very likely think, "You tell me this just because you want to sell insurance." And you don't find yourself convinced enough to buy any insurance at all.

The reason that it fails is because it is too obvious and forcing. When the insurance agent tells the prospect: "You are a good man, so you are supposed to protect your family," it imposes a frame on the prospect that if he does not buy insurance from the agent he is not a good man. Unfortunately, psychologists have found that if you make a strong attempt to change a prospect's attitude to a subject, the prospect will counter with an equally strong response, even if the prospect held a weak attitude prior to the confrontation.

This phenomenon is often encountered by counsellors working with addiction. Research demonstrates that the level of denial faced by the counsellor is highly dependent on his personal counselling style. Arguments, accusations and direct confrontations often lead to strong resistance from the client. On the other hand, using a respectful, reflective approach can usually create motivation for change, and encourage the client to move in a direction desired by the counsellor.

It reminds me of the following fable, which was written by Aesop more than 2,000 years ago. The Wind and the Sun were disputing which was the stronger. Suddenly, they saw a traveller coming down the road. The Sun told the Wind:

"I see a way to settle this dispute: whichever of us can make that traveller take off his cloak shall be regarded as the stronger one." The Wind agreed.

And so the Wind began first. He began to blow as hard as he could upon the traveller. But the harder he blew, the more closely the traveller wrapped his cloak around him. At last the Wind had to give up in despair.

Then the Sun came out and shone in all his glory upon the traveller. He soon found it too hot to walk with his cloak on, and took it off immediately.

In conclusion, the primary mistake of labelling is to appear too imposing so that people think that you are forcing them to change. To avoid this mistake, you should do it in a subtle and indirect way, so that the listener will not find it uncomfortable to make a change. To understand how it can be done, it is useful to consider the making of a classic horror film, *Jaws*.

Directed by Steven Spielberg, *Jaws* is generally considered to be one of the best films ever made. It was the highest-grossing film at the time. In just 78 days after its release, it overtook *The Godfather* – which had until then been the biggest seller of all time at the North American box office – and became the first film ever to reach $100 million in rentals.

However, it was little known that all this success was unexpected, and was inspired by a technical difficulty that almost ruined the film.

The original idea for the production was that the film would be shot with a giant mechanical shark, which was supposed to appear in almost every attack scene. However, this costly, pneumatically powered mechanical shark never worked as designed. Malfunctions happened routinely, and the studio almost shut down production because it became such a pain.

To tackle this problem, Spielberg mostly abandoned the mechanical shark, so that with the exception of the final few minutes, it never appeared at all. Instead, he reverted to the classic Hitchcock approach: the power of suggestion. The presence of the shark was signified indirectly by watery shadows, terrified facial expressions and a scary musical score. Spielberg freely admitted that if Bruce had functioned properly they would not have used the indirect approach; and if they had not used the indirect approach it would not have been such a suspenseful and endlessly frightening film.

The point of the story is that communication is best done in an indirect way. If you want to tell me there is a shark, don't show me the shark directly. Instead, show me all the signs of its ominous presence, and I will be terrified by it. Similarly, if you want to sell me insurance, don't tell me directly why I should buy insurance. Instead, you should talk about something else that will make buying insurance appear important.

However, that leaves a question unanswered: if you should not directly tell the prospect to buy insurance, what should you say instead? To answer this question, let us consider another of Milton Erickson's stories.

Not a Good Christian

One day, when Erickson visited Milwaukee to give a talk, a colleague told him that his aunt had become quite seriously depressed, and he asked Erickson if he could visit her and help her. Erickson agreed, and asked for more details about the man's aunt.

Erickson was told that she had inherited a fortune and lived in the family mansion, but she lived alone and had already lost most of her close relatives. She was in her sixties and had to use a wheelchair, which severely curtailed her social activities. She had begun to hint to her nephew that she was thinking of suicide.

When Erickson arrived at the aunt's home, the old woman was expecting him at the door, and showed him around the house. After a long tour, she ushered Erickson into a greenhouse attached to the house. This was her pride and joy; she had a green thumb, and spent many happy hours working with the plants. She proudly showed him her latest project – taking cuttings from her African violets and starting new plants.

In the discussion that followed, Erickson found out that the woman was very isolated. She had previously been active in her local church, but since her confinement to a wheelchair, she went to church only on Sundays. Since there was no wheelchair access, she always asked someone to lift her into the building only after the service had started, in order not to disrupt the flow of foot traffic into the church. She also insisted on leaving the church before the end of the service for the same reason.

After hearing her story, Erickson told her that her nephew was worried about how depressed she had become. She admitted that it had become quite serious, but she could not really find a way out. At this point, Erickson had already made up his mind how to help this woman. He told her something quite surprising:

"You know, I think your depression is not your real problem. Instead, it is clear to me that the source of your trouble is that you are not being a very good Christian."

She was quite taken aback by this statement. Obviously, if she had insisted on attending the church even in a wheelchair, she could not have been too bad a Christian? She begged Erickson to explain. And he said:

"Here you are with all this money, time on your hands and a green thumb, and it's all going to waste. What I recommend is that you get a copy of your church membership list and then look in the latest church bulletin. You'll find announcements of births, illnesses, graduations, engagements and marriages in there – all the happy and sad events in the life of people in the congregation.

"Make a number of African violet cuttings and get them well established. Then repot them in gift pots and have your handyman drive you to the homes of people who are affected by these happy or sad events. Bring them a plant and your congratulations or condolences and comfort – whichever is appropriate to the situation."

After the explanation, the woman happily concurred that perhaps she had fallen down in her Christian duty, and agreed to do more.

After hearing this story, one of Erickson's students asked him why he had avoided a direct intervention, despite the obvious signs of depression shown by the woman? Why did he just tell her to plant more flowers and give them to the church people?

Erickson explained that he knew that he might only see this woman once, so he had to go for the most direct and powerful solution. To bring about the most substantial change, he had to make use of the things that concerned the woman most. And what concerned her the most?

- She maintained a regular visit to the church despite her mobility problem. It showed that she was actually a very faithful Christian.

- She demonstrated concern for her fellow churchgoers by arriving early and leaving late, so that she would not impede the mobility of others.

- And of course she was proud of her little flowers, yet she did not have enough opportunities to share her hobby with others.

Combining all these, it was simply a logical assignment to ask her to grow flowers and give them to people in the church. So what happened to the lady eventually?

Many years after the visit, there was a feature article in the local newspaper with a large headline, which read: "African Violet Queen of Milwaukee Dies, Mourned by Thousands." The article detailed the life of an incredibly caring woman who had become famous for her trademark flowers and her charitable work with people in the community for 10 years before she died. This woman, of course, was the same depressed aunt who had been labelled by Erickson as a "not very good Christian".

Helping Someone to Die

The above case is very typical of Erickson's ingenuity. He found out whatever was available in the social context of the person, and used it to create a label to change the person's behaviour. Very often, he focused on the "assets" of the person – i.e. something that he or she is very proud of or very concerned about. When he based his suggestions on these "assets", the person could usually find it easier to accept his suggestions, because people often agree with what they like most.

And it was what happened in the story. Compare the following two counselling messages which could have been delivered to the aunt:

- You are a fortunate person with a big house and a lot of money. You should stay positive and treasure a comfortable life.

- You are a good Christian. You are supposed to share your flowers with all your fellow church people.

If you were the aunt in the story, which one would give you more motivation to go on living? Most people will find the second one more powerful. Ironically, the second statement does not even mention phrases such as "stay positive" or "treasure your life". It simply points out something you are good at and like to do, yet once you are reminded of these things, you suddenly want to go on living and enjoy life. Once again, the shark is more powerful when not shown directly.

Therefore, when you try to change a person's behaviour, you should always begin with his primary concerns. This idea applies even when those concerns are actually against your goal. You can sometimes practice a bit of "mental judo" to reframe that initial resistance into a driving force to change the person. Let us consider another Erickson story as an example.

A 21-year-old girl came to Erickson and told him that she wanted to die. She would like to marry someone and have a home and children, but she had never had a boyfriend, and felt that she was destined to be an old maid. She said, "I think I'm too inferior to live. I've got no friends, I stay by myself and I'm too homely to get married. I thought I'd see a psychiatrist before I committed suicide. I'm going to try you for three months, and then if things aren't straightened out that's the end."

Erickson then learned more about the girl. She lived alone and had no social life. Although she had never dated, she did say that a young man at her office showed up at the drinking fountain each time she did, but even though she found him attractive and he made overtures, she ignored him and never spoke to him.

Erickson found that the girl was actually quite pretty, but she managed to make herself unattractive by dressing poorly. She also said she had a gap between her front teeth, which she covered with her hand as she talked. It made her feel extremely insecure about her looks.

When Erickson had finished listening to her, he suggested that since she was going downhill anyway, she had no reason not to enjoy her life before she died. It would be a great idea to take money from her bank account and spend it on whatever she fancied. He told her to go to a department store and ask a woman there to help her select a tasteful outfit, and to a salon to have her hair done properly. The girl agreed to do it, but then Erickson suggested something very strange.

He gave her a task. She was to go home and, in the privacy of her bathroom, practice squirting water through the gap between her front teeth until she could achieve a distance of six feet with accuracy. She thought it was silly, but promised to do it anyway.

When the girl was dressed properly, looking attractive and skilful at squirting water through the gap in her teeth, Erickson made a bizarre suggestion to her. When she went to work the following Monday she had to play a practical joke. She was to show up at the water fountain and wait for the young man to appear. Then she was to take a mouthful of water and squirt it at him through the gap in her teeth.

The girl rejected this idea as impossible, but Erickson asserted that she was going to die anyway, so it did not matter whether it was impossible or not. So the girl agreed to do it.

The next Monday, she went to work dressed in her new outfit and with her hair done. She went to the water fountain, and when the young man approached, she filled her mouth with water and squirted it at him. The young man exclaimed, "You damn little bitch!" This made her laugh, and she dashed away. The young man ran after her and caught her. To her surprise, he grabbed her and they kissed.

The next day, as the young lady approached the water fountain, the young man sprang out from nowhere and sprayed her with a water pistol. Very soon after, they went out to dinner together.

Within a few months she sent Erickson a newspaper clipping announcing her marriage to the young man, and a year later Erickson received a picture of her new baby.

The Insurance Game

The above case demonstrates an approach that appears very unorthodox. Instead of fighting the lady's resistance to live positively, Erickson accepted her wish to die, and used it as an excuse to promote the changes that would be beneficial to her. The girl was also hostile to men, and would not make an effort to be nice to them. Erickson also accepted that, and arranged for her to squirt a man.

You can also apply the same idea to your customers or prospects. Let us go back to the insurance agent example above. What do you do when your prospect believes that life insurance is unimportant? As stated, you cannot just directly tell him that he should care about his family, because in that case you are simply hard-selling. You should accept his resistance and turn it against him.

In my experience, when a prospect tells you that he does not need insurance, there are two common reasons. Firstly, he has not yet come to trust you enough, so he simply rejects everything you say. If this is the case, you should try to build more rapport before you sell to him again.

However, if he still refuses, then he is very likely to be the "money saving" type, who likes to minimise his spending whenever possible, and does not want to "waste" money on something that he does not consider important.

For this kind of person, a great motivator is the possibility of earning a lot of money in a riskless way, and this is the direction that you should follow. So let us come back to the question of how to sell insurance to him? One way to begin the process, paradoxically, is by agreeing with him:

"Yes, you are right – life insurance is really not that important. I would suggest you don't buy it without serious consideration."

And he is sure to be surprised. Again, as stated earlier, the idea is to deliberately say something unusual to capture his attention. After he asks you why, you can tell him:

"Well, most people do not die before sixty after buying a life insurance, so the policy is unlikely to be put into use after all. Actually, this is even better, because his grandsons will get even more money as a result."

And he is bound to be stunned for a second time. Why will his grandsons gain more? Then you can explain:

"You know, buying insurance is actually a game of accumulation. If your grandfather pays a small sum for a life insurance policy of £10,000 for your father, then your father can reinvest this £10,000 as principal, and accumulate £100,000 for you. When you get old, you can in turn buy life insurance with this £100,000, and leave £1,000,000 for your son.

"You see, life insurance is not just about handing over money when you die. If your great grandfather had done something similar, you would have been left a great fortune, so that you could have retired immediately. Better yet, as long as you are patient enough, there is virtually no risk in practising this method.

"So, if you want your children and grandchildren to enjoy the same, it is not unreasonable to invest just a small sum every year, and give them a large sum of riskless profit."

Of course, it is just one of the many possible ways to sell insurance to him, and I am sure there are many better methods out there. However, it is already a lot more persuasive than the earlier version in which you tell him that he should care about his family, because:

1 You have reframed life insurance as something that the prospect can gain no matter whether he dies or not.

2 "If your great grandfather had done something similar, you would have been left a great fortune." You put him in the shoes of his grandchildren, so that he is able to feel the benefit received by the later generations.

3 Following the last point, you also make him feel that, as a man who cares about this family, there is no reason not to do that.

After that, you can begin asking him more about his family situation, and go on with your selling process. By beginning with an opening like this, you can immediately reduce a lot of resistance from the prospect. However, it is still a long way from closing the deal. In the next chapter, you will learn how to continue to increase his desire for your products and services, and make him buy from you in the shortest possible time.

7. Burning Desires

The Making of a Hero

Julius Caesar is one of the great heroes of European history. He was an orator, a historian, a statesman, a lawgiver and an army general. He is known to have never lost a single war, and his conquests extended the territories of Rome to the Atlantic Ocean. As a statesman, he amended several laws for the wellbeing of the general public. He was also a historian, who authored several comprehensive journals about his own military campaigns.

However, what is little known is that Caesar was no more than an ordinary figure when he was in his thirties. Although he was a successful lawyer at that time, he had considerable debts, and was far from the hero that the world remembers. One day, something happened to inspire Caesar to change.

"After reading an episode from the history of Alexander the Great, Caesar sat for a long while, deep in thought, and finally burst into tears. His friends were surprised and asked him the reason. 'Do you think,' said he, 'I have not just cause to weep, when I consider that Alexander at my age had conquered so many nations, and I have all this time done nothing that is memorable?"

The above excerpt is from Plutarch's *Life of Caesar*. Shortly after this outburst of grief for looking inferior to Alexander, he suddenly made a great effort to repay all his debts, and moved on to conquer all the previously independent Spanish tribes with his military feats.

Why was Caesar suddenly so motivated? And what prompted his leap from ordinary to extraordinary? The reason behind his transformation is very simple: he felt bad about himself, so he did everything to get rid of the bad feeling.

In psychology, there is a proposition known as the mood maintenance theory, which states that people do things to maintain a happy, positive mood. If they feel content about their current situation, they are less likely to take risks and ask for more because they do not want to lose what they already have. Conversely, if they are not satisfied with what they have now, they will risk more to improve the situation.

Researcher Zhao Jia-ying of American College Dublin once did an experiment to demonstrate this point. In the experiment, two different groups of participants were made to feel positive and negative emotions respectively, and afterwards asked to perform in a risk-taking situation, to see if there would be any difference observed between them.

In the first part of the experiment, participants had to answer a list of multiple-choice questions, and feedback was given immediately. The feedback, however, was all fabricated. In the "positive" group, they were reported to have given mostly correct answers and only a few wrong ones, whereas the opposite was true in the "negative" group. The idea was to make them feel good and bad about themselves respectively.

They then had to perform in a gambling task. After drawing playing cards from the experimenter, they gained (or lost) points according to the score on each card indicated. For example, if the participant drew a "+1" card, he gained one point, or if he drew a "-1" card, he lost one point. The caveat was that they were allowed to choose between two decks of cards. One deck was the "low risk" deck, in which the positive and negative scores were both low. The other one, naturally, was the "high risk" deck, in which the cards had high risk and high reward.

The result was that the "positive mood" people, who were shown to have given a lot of correct answers in the first part, were more likely to choose the low-risk deck. On the other hand, the "negative mood" people were more likely to take high-risk cards. The reason was that the "negative mood" people did not feel right about themselves, and were more ready to risk more to make up for their "loss" in the first part. In other words, content encourages status quo, whereas discontent promotes changes.

In short, depending on what you want the outcome to be, you should instil different emotions in your target. If you want to inhibit him from making a move, you should remind him how happy he is now, and of the risk of losing it all. However, if you are a salesman or consultant, you will be more likely to want your prospect to feel bad about his current situation, and make a change with your products or services. The question, of course, is how to do it in a practical and effective way.

Beware of the Terrorists!

At the beginning of the 21st century, the aggressive foreign policies of the United States of America had unfortunately instilled hatred of Americans in certain foreign countries. As a result, American tourists and expatriates in those countries often became targets of terrorist assaults.

Against this background, Professor Kahneman of Princeton University devised a little psychological experiment with some American participants. They were divided into two groups. The first group of participants were asked: "Suppose you are going to make a trip to a foreign country, how much you would spend on an insurance that would cover death of any kind?" And the participants had to tell the experimenter how much insurance they would buy for themselves.

The second group were asked an almost identical question, but with one change. Instead of covering "any kind of death", they were offered another insurance that just covered "death in a terrorist attack". Logically, "death of any kind" includes more than just "death in a terrorist attack", so the insurance in the first group should be worth more than the one in the second group.

Nevertheless, the experiment result showed the opposite. People in the second group were willing to pay more for the insurance than those in the first group. In other words, the "terrorist only" insurance sold better than the "death of any kind" one. Why would people pay more for something that was actually worth less?

The reason is simple: people "think" more with emotions than reason. "Death of any kind" is not emotional enough to make people associate it with something fearful. On the other hand, the term "terrorist attack" triggered the fear of being kidnapped or murdered in a foreign country, and the emotion of fear was more motivating than a logical calculation of risk – and that was why the second group of people wanted to pay more.

The lesson from the experiment is that the ability to sell a product is not about how good the product is, but about how much you can make the prospect feel that they need it. This is easy to understand, but few can actually apply it.

When it comes to introducing your products, there are two prevailing and related concepts in the market. The first one is called unique selling propositions (USP), which refer to anything unique about your product or services. For example, Domino's Pizza once offered a 30-minute delivery service, and failure to achieve that would make the pizza free. This was something unique among the competition, so they simply used that idea as their slogan: "Thirty Minutes or Free!" (Unfortunately, it no longer offers this deal, because the promise caused a number of traffic accidents, so today it is nothing more than a slogan.)

Another related concept is called value proposition. It means to distil what you can bring to the customer in one short, simple sentence. For instance, the courier company FedEx once used the slogan: "When it absolutely, positively has to be there overnight." It highlights the primary benefit of the company: it can deliver things swiftly and safely when it is necessary.

There is nothing wrong with these two concepts. However, if you are in a face-to-face situation, or if you already have some prior knowledge about your targets, you can say something better than those generic slogans, because, like the "death of any kind" insurance, it is too unspecified to arouse people. So how can you personalise your messages so that they can make people feel something immediately? Let us consider the following information.

Witch in the Cupboard

One of the most common characteristics of mental disorders is black-and-white thinking. Patients who suffer from this always see things as all-or-nothing. They can shift from idealising situations to feeling completely hopeless in an instant. They alternate between high regard and heavy disappointment like a yo-yo.

The reason they think like this is because they suffer from a mental distortion called over-generalisation. When they see a little improvement, they will think that there is great hope. On the other hand, when they have a little disappointment, they will think it is the end of the world, and they are completely hopeless. In other words, they magnify the consequences of everything that happens to them.

It is very easy to sell your products to these kind of people, because if they feel good about your products they will exaggerate their benefits, and buy them without much thinking. But of course, most of your prospects are normal people, and they are unlikely to be affected by such extreme emotions, and buy from you so hastily. So the question is: is it possible to instil such overwhelming emotions in your prospects and give them an urge to buy? In order to answer this question, let us consider the following story:

Tom is a 10-year-old boy who has trouble sleeping because he thinks there is a witch hiding in his wardrobe, who waits until he falls asleep, opens the door slightly and then watches him silently.

Tom becomes very afraid of going to bed, so he asks his mother for help. His mother tells him:

"We know the witch. Her name is Lily, and she is a gentle and lonely witch. She's been there for a long time. She wants to play with your toys, but she is too afraid of showing herself. Say 'Goodnight Lily' before going to bed, and she'll forget about playing and go to bed too."

After that, whenever Tom goes to bed, he says to the wardrobe, "Goodnight, Lily!" and he sleeps well.

Tom's fear of the witch was eliminated because his mother transformed a horrible identity (witch) into a behavioural description (someone who wants to play with your toy). Once you move from the subjective perception of identity to the objective observation of behaviour, you will become detached from the situation, and minimise the interference of emotions.

One psychotherapist also uses a similar approach to deal with her patients, like those people with extreme mood swings, as described earlier. Suppose a man comes to see her and says: "No one likes me. I want to kill myself," the first thing she will do is to ask him:

"How do you know that no one likes you?"

And the patient may reply:

"I give advice to my clients, but they don't listen to me."

Then the psychotherapist may say:

"So you think they must follow what you say after consulting you?"

"Well, at least they should give serious thought to that."

"And how do you know they have not given it serious thought?"

"I know because they do the exact opposite the very next day."

"So you mean they take you seriously only if they do exactly what you say the next day?"

"No, but they should not do the opposite so quickly."

"Have you ever investigated the exact reason for why they pursued something different instead?"

"Well, not really."

"Then how do you know their reason for doing the opposite was because they didn't listen to you?"

"Well, I…"

"Is it possible that they have already considered your idea seriously, but due to some other concerns unknown to you, they had to do the opposite?"

"That's not impossible, I confess."

"So perhaps they still value your opinion a lot, but they are just forced to do it in another way."

In the above example, the psychotherapist changes the mind of the patient by boiling down the generalisation: "They hate me" into a behavioural description of facts: "They did the opposite of my recommendation", and then seeks an alternative explanation to the fact. Similar to the witch story above, once you separate identity from behaviour, you can eliminate unnecessary emotions.

In other words, in order to eliminate undesirable emotions from anyone, you can follow these steps known as the Three A's:

1 Ask for Specifics: deconstruct the generalisation, and find out what facts it is based on.

2 Attack the Assumptions: challenge the validity of the generalisation.

3 Alter the Explanation: provide a more harmless account which induces less emotion.

So this is how you can help your friends to deal with psychological problems, and it is also useful in situations such as handling complaints. However, when it comes to selling, this is not very appropriate. As explained earlier, instead of removing emotions from the prospect, we actually want to make him emotional, to get him to buy as soon as possible. In order to do it, you simply have to reverse the process.

The Ugly T-Shirt

I once met a client who was a fashion designer. She was wearing a very ugly t-shirt. The colour was far from traditional, and it had a very eccentrically designed pocket. I reasoned that no shop would sell such a horrible-looking t-shirt, so it must be her own design. So at some point in the conversation I pretended to be intrigued, and pointed to her and said, "It is strange..."

"What's that?" She looked confused.

"It looked quite special..."

"What are you talking about?" She was anxious to hear my explanation.

"This t-shirt you are wearing is the most creative one I have ever seen. The colour created a special sense of wildness. And not only that, the pocket there has a very extraordinary design. Where did you buy that?"

That fashion designer immediately became an orator and came up with paragraph after paragraph about the t-shirt. As I expected, she said that she had designed it herself, but many people had expressed the opinion that it was just too eccentric.

I was not surprised by that, but I still licked her boots, and told her that those people who said that must be too old to appreciate its innovation. I immediately got her tremendous rapport, and I eventually got her to buy a savings plan from me.

Why did she suddenly like me a lot? It was because I happened to give her confidence in her weakest link. No one is happy when he is praised for his obvious strength, because he hears it far too often, and compliments are like common goods – they devalue with a large supply.

So, when you praise someone, you should always go for the undervalued areas, because it is where they feel the most sensitive, and need the maximum approval. When people hear that, they will immediately find you a lot different from most others, and feel that you understand them well.

The above story teaches you the three basic steps with which you can quickly instil emotions in your customers, which could be summarised as the Three I's:

1 Identify: find out the problems on which you can build emotions, and it is best if it is something that they care most about.

2 Intensify: frame the situation on an emotional level, which has a direct implication for their self-image.

3 Idolise: make it clear that he is right and the world is wrong, and blame any problem or failure on other people. (Or do the opposite if you want to infuriate him instead.)

You can also apply it to your sales process. Suppose you are a salesman for an Internet provider. You have just approached a prospect, and he has told you that his Internet speed is too slow, so that it takes him too long to download DVD rip files. After you hear this, do not just blurt out your so-called "value propositions":

"We provide a fast Internet connection at a low price, which will allow you to enjoy a high-speed connection with the cheapest price in town. We are offering this because we are a brand-new company, and our technology is much more advanced than those of many existing providers. If you can sign up with us now, you can enjoy a special discount for the first six months."

The above "value propositions" are too generic to apply to any specific prospect, and therefore are not powerful enough to get him interested immediately. Instead, you should try something like this:

"We provide a fast Internet connection at a low price, which will allow you to download a DVD rip in just twenty minutes. If you continue to use your current provider, you will waste a lot of time in downloading stuff when you can get it faster – and surely it is not a reasonable service for a respected customer like you. However, this is not your fault, because you have just simply chosen a bad provider."

The second paragraph can usually generate much more interest, and some people may even go into a rant about all the problems they are having with their existing provider. Why is it more effective? The reason is simply that while the first paragraph is all about the company, the second paragraph is actually about the prospect himself. People just want to talk about themselves, so that if you can relate your benefits to their current situation, they will immediately be very much interested in you.

However, this is nothing more than just the starting point. Getting an initial interest is far from closing the deal. You have to magnify the emotions to make him go from "feel like having it" to "must have it", and this is one of the most challenging parts in the sales process. In order to understand how to do it, let us consider the following information.

Rekindle the Fire

People often think that they will be happy when they are able to get the things they want, such as a big house, a new car, a good job, more money and so on. However, the truth is that these will only be enough to keep them happy for a while.

For example, the first time a man owns a brand new sports car, he may be very happy. He feels very satisfied when others admire him driving such a car.

Yet a month or two later, this enthusiasm usually disappears, and he will treat it as "just another car."

In psychology, this is called habituation, which refers to the gradual decrease of emotional reaction once a form of stimulus becomes familiar. This phenomenon is often seen in couples. When they are on their honeymoon they very much enjoy being with each other. However, after a while, the relationship can become boring and the chemistry dies out. Many couples know that they have this problem, but they do not know how to rekindle the fire that they once had.

So how can you tackle the problem? You do not have to buy a new car every month or find a new wife every year. You just have to prevent yourself from getting used to the relationship, as the following demonstrates.

In 2008, psychologist James Graham conducted a study to see how couples bond to each other. He followed 20 couples over a period of time by asking them to carry digital devices with them during their normal daily activities. Occasionally, they had to answer a few questions about their mood and how they felt toward their partners via text messages. After more than 1,000 of these buzz-report-introspect-text moments, he looked over the data and tried to find out how their daily events affected their relationships.

The result was that couples who have strong bonding usually go through different challenges together. Challenges are generally seen as putting pressure on people, but instead they actually strengthen their bonds, because each time they overcome a challenge, it brings them a joy in success which makes them feel happy together. This ongoing adventure gives the couple a continuous sense of thrill and excitement, and bonds them together in the voyage of life.

In other words, happy marriage is not about couples having everything they want and "living happily ever after", because no matter how "happy" they get, they will still get used to it after a period of time. Instead, the secret of a happy relationship is the continuous process of first depriving them of what they want, and then giving it to them only after they have made a combined effort to get it. In other words, without disappointment, there is no satisfaction either.

In order to go forward, you first have to go backward. It is similar to the way that a kid plays on a swing in the playground. When he begins, the first thrust that he makes is usually not very high. However, after the first move forward, he swings himself backward to gather momentum to swing forward again. The second forward swing usually goes higher than the first one. Then he swings back again to prepare for the third thrust. The process continues until he goes up to where he wants.

It is the same with emotional arousal. Normally, if you want to make people feel happy about a certain object, you will keep telling them the good things about it. This is what most salespeople and marketers do. However, as explained earlier, the listeners may soon become habituated to what you say, and suspect whether you are hiding the bad side from them. How can you overcome this problem? Let us consider the following example.

Push and Pull

Suppose you are an independent author who is looking for a suitable platform to publish your book. You come across an advertisement from a self-publishing company called CreateSpake. The advertisement says:

"The online bookstore of CreateSpake has nearly 20 million active customers. Even if just one in 20 of them buys your book, you will still be able to sell a million copies.

"In addition, we are very cheap to begin with. There is no start-up fee at all, and we also provide a free worldwide distribution network. You will be able to enjoy one of the largest distribution channels in the world without paying a penny.

"Moreover, we offer professional services to help you in designing and marketing the book, so that even if you are new to publishing, you will still be able to publish like a professional with minimum knowledge."

To be fair, the above advertisement is not too bad a piece of copywriting, as it outlines the most important advantages of the company in a very short paragraph. However, there is one major problem with this advertisement: it keeps pulling without pushing. As we learned earlier, it is more effective to push people away before you pull them towards you. To make it more effective, you can change it into this:

"The greatest challenge for an author is not to write the book itself, but to find readers to read it. Even if you have written a very good book, it will be useless if no one buys it.

"The online bookstore of CreateSpake has nearly 20 million active customers. Even if just one in 20 of them buys your book, you will still be able to sell a million copies.

"Nevertheless, publishing a book has costs. Firstly, there is usually a charge for handling the files and buying your ISBN. Then there is also an annual distribution cost that you have to pay every year."

"Fortunately, we are very cheap to begin with. All the above-mentioned fees are waived, and we also provide a free worldwide distribution network. You will be able to enjoy one of the largest distribution channels in the world without paying a penny.

"However, not every book can sell well. People often judge a book by its layout. If your design is not professional enough, people will dismiss your work as amateurish. In addition, you still need to spend a lot of time advertising your book.

"This is where we come into play. We offer professional services to help you in designing and marketing the book, so that even if you are new to publishing, you will still be able to publish like a professional with minimum knowledge."

Most people find the second version better than the first one. The major difference in the second is that each time, before presenting an advantages of the company, it scares you with a common difficulty faced by an independent author. By doing so, it achieves three things:

1 Firstly, it provides a context of why their service is valuable. You cannot call a person tall without having a short person to compare with. Similarly, the readers

cannot feel great about your company without knowing that they cannot get the same if they do not choose you.

2 Secondly, it creates a more complete picture of the situation in the whole industry. As explained in the second chapter, the more details you can give, the more people will feel that you are experienced and trustworthy.

3 Most importantly, it makes you fear before it gives you hope. As explained, it makes your selling points even more appealing by putting the listeners on an emotional rollercoaster.

To summarise, this method of presentation consists of the following three steps, which could be known as the Three P's:

1 Polarise: divide the situation into two categories (e.g. buying and not buying).

2 Pair: associate all the good feelings to the desired direction (i.e. buying) and the bad ones to the opposite (i.e. not buying).

3 Push-and-pull: present in alternation, i.e. good, bad, good, bad, and good, etc.

With this, you will be able to drive up the emotions of your listener through a series of intermitted ups and downs. It is not only essential for building up their desire for your products, but also useful in helping you to close the deal.

Less is More

Very often, salespeople have no problem in getting the attention of the prospect, or making them interested in what they offer. However, when it comes to the final point of closing, they often meet the maximum resistance from the prospect. It is usually due to the fact that the prospect has to consider: "Do I really need his products?" And this is the crucial time, when the fate of the whole sales process is decided.

Usually, there are two approaches to deal with this. The first approach is to be firm and try to muscle it through. Suppose it's a financial adviser who is trying to sell a fund to his client, the adviser will say something like: "Don't worry, the fund is very safe! The fund has operated for over ten years, and they have a very good reputation, and..." And he will go on to repeat the selling points again and again until the client buys from him.

The advantage of this approach is that it sometimes works. When a person becomes indecisive, he is usually very susceptible, so that just a small push is enough to make him decide. However, if the client is the stronger type who does not like to be pushed around, then this tactic may simply backfire, because it activates his reverse psychology and makes him refuse to buy immediately.

This is why salespeople may sometimes try another approach. They try to appear to be generous and considerate, and tell the client: "Please don't make the decision so soon. Think carefully before you decide to buy." The good thing is that clients with big egos usually find this more comfortable to hear. Unfortunately, there is an obvious danger that you let your client off the hook, and he may never come back again to buy.

If both approaches have their respective weaknesses, what should you do then? The best idea is to combine both approaches, and use them in alternation in a push-and-pull process as described above. To begin with, you should avoid appearing too forcing, because it may alarm the prospect. Instead, you should give him an illusion of control by first pushing him away. Using the financial adviser example above, when the client is considering whether he should buy it, the adviser may say:

"It is good to think carefully before you invest in anything, because there is always a cost in investing, i.e. you have to lock away a part of your cash. Therefore, if you really need 100 per cent of your cash very urgently, then you should not invest any money in the fund."

Most of the time your client will say, "Well not really, I don't need all my cash at the moment." And now you should go on to exaggerate the "reason" for not investing:

"No, I am serious. I want you to be happy with your decision. Unless you see an advantage in investing your money, you should just put it in a bank, as there is no safer way than keeping it there."

Usually, the client will show less resistance at this point, because you have already exaggerated the "reason" not to invest a lot. In other words, it is reverse psychology. After that, you can try to pull him back:

"Nevertheless, I want to point out the opportunity cost of not investing. As explained, you can easily make seven per cent a year in this fund. If you hold and compound it for ten years more, you can already double your cash. Twenty years later, you can quadruple it. And forty years later… guess what? Your cash will grow fifteen-fold!"

After outlining the advantage of investing, you should push him away again:

"But of course, there is no investment that has no risk. In fact, this fund fell by about twenty three per cent in the 2008 crash, despite an averaged return of sixteen per cent over the last twenty years. However, I understand that some people would rather have safety than long-term gains. If you are really afraid of fluctuations, you should consider putting your money in time deposits with absolute safety, even though, under the current low-interest environment it only gives you two per cent per annum."

Then you pull him back again:

"However, you are just twenty-five now, and you still have a lot of years ahead of you. Imagine if you travelled back to twenty years ago and bought this fund, how much compound interest you would have earned with sixteen per cent every year? If you decide to do nothing now, then all your coming years for compounding your money would be wasted."

Finally, you push him away one more time:

"But again, I am not suggesting that you invest everything you have. At the moment your monthly income after tax is £1,500. I know that as a young man you have to spend a lot of money to hang out with friends, date girls and do many other things, so it would not be a good idea to invest too much every month – I think it would not be too much for you if you were just to invest £100 every month."

Of course, investing just £100 of £1,500 is far too little, but you deliberately say this because most of the time the prospect will reply, "No, I think I can do more than that." If his reaction is positive, then you can go on to close the deal:

"I also think that you should save more than just £100 a month. As you grow older you will have more burdens such as family and children. The more you invest now, the more you will get in the future. If you can start with a little more today, you will make your future much easier. Do you want to invest a smaller amount of £150, or a more reasonable one such as £250?"

And, if you have really done your persuasion well before reaching this closing stage, your client will usually invest the larger amount you suggested.

The key to this technique is that when you push him away, you should exaggerate the possible reasons for rejection to make it look ridiculous. On the other hand, when you pull him back, you should bring out your suggestions in a subtle and objective way, so that he will not find you hard-selling, and will think that what you say may actually make sense.

The reason for doing this is that the human mind strives for equilibrium. When something is understated, we tend to speak for it and bolster it up, and vice versa. Suppose you are very good at tennis, and your friend points that out to other players in front of you. However he makes an exaggeration like this:

"You know, my friend is a very good tennis player! There was once a tennis coach who said that if he had turned professional, he could have won as many Grand Slam titles as Roger Federer. Even without any practice, he can easily beat any professional on the tour in straight sets."

Unless you are really as good as he describes, you will try to appear humble: "No, no, I am actually not that good. Sometimes I make double faults when I serve, and my volleys are my biggest weakness."

On the other hand, if your friend completely underestimates you: "His tennis is so bad. Even a beginner can beat him," then you may get a bit angry and assert that you are not a very bad player after all.

This is the same in the above example. For instance, one of the most common rejections for saving money is "need cash." By exaggerating them as in the above example (i.e. "Don't invest if you need 100 per cent of your cash"), it makes the prospect feel that perhaps he does not really need so much cash after all.

On the other hand, when you try to pull him back, you should tune down your pitch, and suggest it indirectly through the use of universal truths and future projections. For example, when you tell him about the advantage of saving money, you say: "Imagine if you travelled back to twenty years ago and bought this fund, how much compound interest you would have earned with sixteen per cent every year?" It gets him to realise the importance of starting investing early, so that he will think that it is not a bad idea to invest after all.

In conclusion, if you want to destroy a belief, you should overstate it to a point until it looks ridiculous. Conversely, if you want to strengthen a belief, you should understate its importance, so that the listener will try to justify it himself. If you can combine this idea with the push-and-pull method outlined earlier, then there will be no one to whom you cannot sell.

Finally, we have reached the last chapter, where you will find a comprehensive example of what you have learned throughout the book. It was mentioned in the first chapter that Scarlett somehow managed to persuade a very difficult customer to buy a very expensive jacket in the shop. In the next chapter you will see exactly how it happened.

8. Mrs. McKinsey Bought

Closing a Difficult Deal

In the boutique where Scarlett worked, there was a very stingy customer called Mrs. McKinsey. She was never generous, and always haggled. Although she visited the shop every now and then, she never really bought anything there. Instead, she just chatted with the people there as a pastime for a housewife. In particular, she always liked to talk about her daughter with Scarlett, because they were of a similar age.

One day, Mrs. McKinsey was chatting with Scarlett in the shop as usual, and she revealed something interesting to her.

"You know, my daughter's birthday is coming soon," said Mrs. McKinsey.

"Indeed? Are you going to buy anything for her then?" asked Scarlett.

"Well, she will soon be starting her summer intern job in a big company. I think I will buy her some clothes for that." But then Mrs. McKinsey added: "However, I am not going to buy anything here, because your clothes are so expensive."

As always, Mrs. McKinsey was very candid about her preference for low prices. Scarlett did not bother to argue with her.

"Yes, our clothes are slightly more expensive than other shops, as their quality is taken into account," said Scarlett. "Regardless of that, I think your daughter will be happy to know that you are buying her some new clothes."

"I don't think so! She never appreciates anything I do for her! Young people nowadays do not listen to their parents anymore! Do you listen to your mum?"

Scarlett had talked to Mrs. McKinsey before, and she knew that she did not get along well with her daughter. After all, she could not imagine who would like having a mother like Mrs. McKinsey. Nevertheless, Scarlett suddenly had an idea about how to continue the conversation, so she said:

"I do listen to her, but I don't like her buying me clothes. As a matter of fact, the more clothes she buys me, the more uncomfortable I feel."

"Oh, why's that?" Mrs. McKinsey was curious.

"Because the clothes she buys me make me feel like a monster," said Scarlett.

"What do you mean?" asked Mrs. McKinsey.

Then Scarlett told her a story:

"I still remember – it was my first summer job interview just before university. It was a very competitive position with a lot of people applying for it. I was supposed to wear something like a suit. However, one week before the interview, I found that I had grown tall so that the old ones didn't fit any more. My mum said she would buy me a new one.

"However, I knew that she had no fashion sense, so she was bound to buy me something that would make me look like a monster. So I taught her two very efficient ways to choose the best clothes."

"And what are those ways?" asked Mrs. McKinsey.

"The first way is to go on to an online forum and ask them. However, if you do not use the Internet, another idea is to simply go to different boutiques and ask the people there. You have to go to those shops with a higher-end target market because they are usually better-informed."

And Scarlett continued with her story: "In the end, my mum bought me something that I really like. It also impressed the interviewer on that day, as she said that it was rare to find an undergrad girl who dressed so maturely. I eventually got that job against a great deal of competition."

"That's very nice," said Mrs. McKinsey.

"Yes, so when you buy clothes you always have to buy the right ones. Talking about that, have you got any idea what to buy for your daughter?"

"Well, regrettably not yet."

"Then you'd better figure that out! There's no better way to make people happy than giving gifts, but if what you buy is not what they want, you'll waste your time and money. Does your daughter look extremely happy when you buy her things?"

"Very seldom!"

"This is exactly what I am talking about. If you are not aware of what the latest trend is, then you will very easily make the wrong decision and buy the wrong things. However, there comes another problem."

"What problem is that?" asked Mrs. McKinsey.

"Trendy clothes are usually more expensive. It is, of course, not a good idea to spend too much unnecessary money. However, there is a simple method that can get you the latest fashion with minimum cost."

"Really? What's the method?" Mrs. McKinsey could not resist learning a way to save money.

"The method is to just buy a good jacket instead of the whole suit. Jackets play a very important role in female attire. A good jacket can convey a sense of maturity and trendiness. It will be particular useful for a high-class workplace."

Then Scarlett continued: "I believe your daughter is as intelligent as you, so she must have a summer job in a respectable company. Can you tell me, what kind of company is it?"

"It's a mutual fund. I used many connections to get her there," answered Mrs. McKinsey, and she felt a bit happy to be praised.

"I see. In that case, there are two kinds of jackets that are particularly suitable for these companies." Then Scarlett dragged Mrs. McKinsey aside and showed her two jackets. "The first one is an open-front jacket, and it is one of the most fashionable items. It allows a different combination of colours so that you can look great with whatever you wear."

Then Scarlett picked up another jacket: "Another choice is a lapel blazer. It is a glamorous item that exudes an aura of maturity. It is particularly good for young people, because it can make them look more professional."

Then she continued: "If your daughter is going to work in a mutual fund, then I think this lapel blazer will be more suitable. People usually dress conservatively in finance jobs. This blazer will be closer to the dressing culture in a mutual fund."

But then she added: "However, there is one more reason why your daughter should get this blazer."

"Why?"

"I also have a friend who has worked as an intern in a fund before," said Scarlett. "According to her, if you are a girl there is one thing you must pay particular attention to."

"What is that?" asked Mrs. McKinsey.

"That's appearance," said Scarlett. "Female graduates usually end up working on the marketing side, where one must know how to present a professional image to the customers. The marketing head usually picks people by the way they look. If she finds that you just dress yourself with random and cheap clothes, you will strike her as being not very presentable.

"On the other hand, if she sees that you know how to dress yourself adequately and professionally, they are much more likely to hire you permanently after you graduate."

Scarlett continued: "This is why if your daughter has a jacket like this, it will be a great help to her, because an internship is an essential stepping stone to a good career."

However, Scarlett then changed her tone. "Nevertheless, I will not suggest that you buy it right away."

"Why is that?" asked Mrs. McKinsey.

"I know you are a very economical person, who always has to consider the price. Even though this jacket is certainly very useful, I am not sure whether or not you are willing to spend this much – even when it's for your daughter."

"Well, I..."

"It is never a good idea to spend unwisely," said Scarlett. "If your goal is to save money, you can just buy her something cheaper. Even though your daughter may not like it as much as this jacket, you can save more money if you buy one of the cheaper ones."

"Well, I'm not always that strict about money," said Mrs. McKinsey. Obviously, she was not quite comfortable to be labelled as a stingy woman.

"Still, you should not buy it if you do not recognise the benefits it brings. By spending just a little more, you will be able to give your daughter what she really needs, and it will be something she really appreciates. This may not be the first priority of yours, but it is something to be taken into account. When was the last time your daughter looked really happy with what you've bought her?"

That made Mrs. McKinsey think deeply. Apparently, Scarlett's strategy of utilising the strained relationship between Mrs. McKinsey and her daughter was working. Scarlett continued:

"However, even though it may not be an easy decision to spend more, I can assure you that this jacket is a good one. It is designed by our owner, Mr. Thomson, who was a famous designer before he retired, and it cannot be found elsewhere. If your daughter doesn't like it you can still sell it online for a high price, because it is not a commonly seen item."

After hearing that, Mrs. McKinsey's concerned expression lifted significantly. Scarlett knew what she was thinking. She grabbed her customer's arm and said:

"We are doing a discount right now. If you buy it today, it will be even cheaper," said Scarlett. "Please come this way and let me wrap it up for you."

And that was how Mrs. McKinsey bought the blazer from Scarlett.

Post-Mortem Analysis

Let us analyse the above story. While it is impossible to avoid a customer who appears difficult at first, sometimes she may subsequently reveal information that creates selling opportunities.

In the story above, Scarlett discovered that Mrs. McKinsey's daughter had a birthday coming up soon, and used that fact to suggest to her that she buy things for her. However, Mrs. McKinsey rejected the idea immediately:

"I am not going to buy anything here, because your clothes are so expensive."

Whenever a customer gives you a rejection, especially at such an early stage, it is important to remember not to argue with them. Instead, you should get them to continue to talk about themselves, in order to create more chances for you to open them up. Scarlett replied:

"Yes, our clothes are slightly more expensive than other shops, as their quality is taken into account. Regardless of that, I think your daughter will be happy to know that you are buying her some new clothes."

Scarlett just gave a very short reply to Mrs. McKinsey's criticism, and moved on to encourage her to talk. The customer then mentioned that her daughter never appreciated anything she bought her. It reminded Scarlett that Mrs. McKinsey and her daughter did not get along well. It opened up a "weakness" in her psyche: her parental need to be loved by her daughter. So how could she take advantage of that?

The first thing she did was to get Mrs. McKinsey's attention. When the customer asked her whether she listened to her mother, she deliberately replied with a strange answer:

"I do listen to her, but I don't like her buying me clothes. As a matter of fact, the more clothes she buys me, the more uncomfortable I feel."

And when Mrs. McKinsey asked why, she said:

"Because the clothes she buys me make me feel like a monster."

As explained in the fourth chapter, it got the attention of Mrs. McKinsey, and made her curious enough to listen to what she had to say. Scarlett then told a story about herself. On the surface, it was about how she had bought a suit for an interview, but in fact it was subtly communicating two messages to the customer:

1 You do not know about what young people like to wear. You have to ask professionals like us.

2 You should not be too penny-pinching when buying clothes for your daughter, because good clothes would make her look good in her job.

As demonstrated in the fifth chapter, telling a story is always the most efficient, economical and engaging weapon of persuasion. It put Mrs. McKinsey into a mindset that her priority should be helping her daughter in her job, instead of saving money. In other words, there is a practical justification for a little extra spending on clothes for her daughter. Later, you saw how Scarlett went along this line to continue the sale process.

After the story, Scarlett immediately asked Mrs. McKinsey whether she knew what her daughter wanted, and Mrs. McKinsey confessed that she really had no idea. As explained in the third chapter, the purpose of asking this was to make her acknowledge her lack of knowledge, which reminded her that she really needed Scarlett's help.

If she were to make suggestions immediately, the customer might feel a bit uncomfortable and think: "How can you be sure that I cannot buy what she likes? And why are you so sure that what you offer is what she wants?"

On the other hand, if you can first get the customer to acknowledge that her daughter really didn't like what she bought very much, then your suggestion will have a stronger impact, because she has already recognised what you say is true.

When Scarlett did this, she employed a little trick that you learned in a previous chapter. She began the question with a universal truth:

"There's no better way to make people happy than giving gifts, but if what you buy is not what they want, you'll waste your time and money. Does your daughter look extremely happy when you buy her things?"

And Mrs. McKinsey said that it was true. However, common sense would tell you that most adolescents are rebellious and do not usually appreciate what parents do for them. In addition, Scarlett already knew that, because the customer had just revealed it. After getting confirmation from the customer, she continued:

"This is exactly what I am talking about. If you are not aware of what the latest trend is, then you will very easily make the wrong decision and buy the wrong things."

After pulling the customer a step closer to her goal, however, Scarlett pushed her away a little:

"However, there comes another problem. Trendy clothes are usually more expensive. It is of course not a good idea to spend too much unnecessary money. However, there is a simple method that can get you the latest fashion with minimum cost."

The purpose of this was to address a possible rejection even before it came into the customer's mind. In Mrs. McKinsey's case, it was about money, money and money. As explained in the last chapter, it is a good idea to first deal with her possible concerns upfront, because it can minimise her resistance later. It also makes you appear to understand the customer's concerns very well.

Then Scarlett began the actual process of selling products. She showed Mrs. McKinsey two very fashionable jackets, and compared the features of each of them. As explained in the second chapter, the purpose of doing this was to avoid the impression of hard-selling any particular item. Instead, she was giving her a number of options, and chose the best one for her according to her needs. It not only showed that she knew a lot about the latest fashion, but also made her recommendation appeared fair.

After introducing the jackets, Scarlett began to relate them to the benefits for Mrs. McKinsey's daughter. No matter how great a product is, no one will ever buy it unless they can see what it can do for them. By pointing out the importance of professional image in the working world, Scarlett reinforced the idea that Mrs. McKinsey should spend a bit more money to help her daughter to find a better career.

Now here is the most interesting part. Usually, when a salesman sees some positive reaction from the customer, he will press on to try to close the deal. However, it was not what Scarlett did, and she did not continue to explain how great the jacket was, either. Instead, she told Mrs. McKinsey not to buy it right away.

This paradoxical action achieved two things. Firstly, it created a curious moment, and it made the listener want to hear what she was going to say. Secondly, and more importantly, it avoided running into the reverse psychology of the customer. As explained in the last chapter, the more you push the customer to buy something, the more you risk a rejection, because everyone likes to make their own choice, and no one likes to be forced to do anything.

Instead, if you agree with their reasons for rejection, and exaggerate them to an inappropriate extent, then they will strangely want to disagree with the rejection, and try to persuade themselves to buy.

This is especially important for a challenging customer like Mrs. McKinsey, as she had already raised a rejection right at the beginning – that she thought the price was expensive. By agreeing with her that it really was not very cheap, Scarlett showed that she had listened to her, and was not trying to force her to do anything.

That being said, Scarlett immediately bought the attention back to her daughter. She asked Mrs. McKinsey to consider two "choices." She could either save money by buying something cheap, or spend a little more to help her daughter. It put the customer into a dilemma: do you love money, or do you love your daughter? Even for a woman like Mrs. McKinsey, it was hard to accept that she was a "bad mother" who would rather save money than give the best to her daughter. It put a lot of "ethical pressure" on her to buy the jacket.

After that, Scarlett released the pressure a bit by helping her to rationalise the decision. She pointed out that even though the blazer was more expensive than usual, it was compensated for by the fact that it could be sold online for a high price. It implied that there was already a "safety net" to the price issue, so that Mrs. McKinsey had no reason not to buy it immediately. It helped Mrs. McKinsey to overcome her final critical factor, and she eventually bought the jacket.

An Unfair World

One year after the Mrs. McKinsey story, Scarlett left Mr. Thomson's employment, as she had completed her degree with first-class honours. After graduation, she joined a prestigious multinational firm as a management trainee, following a gruelling selection process. Her skills in communication were more than helpful in her job, and she went on to enjoy a very successful time in that company.

Everyone wants to have a smooth and successful career path, but only a few actually manage it. In the modern world, despite a dramatic improvement in our living standards, many people's satisfaction with their lives seems to go the other way. Hundreds of years ago you could live comfortably on your own without any professional qualifications. You could earn a reasonable income without working overtime. You could build yourself a happy home without worrying about your mortgage. However, this is no longer feasible in the society in which you are living now.

The competition in the modern capitalist society is enormous. Your career path does not even begin at the point when you go out to work. It is already decided way back in your childhood. Only if you do well in your school can you go to a good university; and only if you go to a good university can you find a great job and earn a lot of money. The day you were born into this world you were already entering a rat race.

While there are quite a few winners in the race, it is far more common to see people in the other category. It is not just a matter of personal ego, but also a practical financial problem. Why are consumer prices rising like a rocket when your salary remains stationary? Why do you have to pay for your house, your car and other things when you have virtually nothing left after that? Why are there some people who can buy multiple properties without blinking an eye, when you have to hesitate to purchase a new mobile phone?

It may not seem very fair to suggest this, but equal effort does not lead to equal results. Some people believe that hard work can bring them a better life. They often cite the case of Thomas Edison, who had failed many times before he invented the light bulb. However, even though it is true that Edison worked very hard to succeed, what is little known is that the light bulb was actually not his invention at all.

The Light Bulb Battle

Contrary to what has been taught in schools for years, Thomas Edison neither invented the light bulb, nor held the first patent for its modern design. Light bulbs already existed 50 years before Edison's 1879 patent. Moreover, Sir Joseph Swan from England had obtained the first patent for the same light bulb in Britain one year prior to Edison's patent date. Edison's light bulb was, in fact, just a carbon copy of Swan's.

As a matter of fact, Edison was very much the underdog at the beginning of the light bulb battle. Even though he did try to register a patent and profit from it, Sir Joseph was obviously unhappy about it, so he took Edison to Court for patent infringement. In the end, Edison lost and the Court forced him, as part of the settlement, to name Swan as a partner in his electric company. Eventually, Edison managed to acquire all of Swans' interest in the newly renamed Edison and Swan United Electric Company.

Edison fared no better back home in the States, as the Patent Office ruled that Edison's patents were invalid because he had based them upon the earlier work of another chap named William Sawyer. To make it worse, Swan had sold his U.S. patent rights, in June 1882, to another company, so that Edison lost all his rights on both sides of the Atlantic.

So, how come Edison eventually came to be remembered as the father of the light bulb? It all came down to his ability as a businessman. If Sir Joseph had beaten him in terms of inventing speed, Edison was clearly superior in his marketing ability. Basically, he went into the business of setting up a DC power distribution network in New York City, and selling a new kind of light bulb that used this electricity. This process was facilitated by aggressive marketing efforts that focused on the low cost of this form of power. It worked well in the end, and Edison's client base rapidly expanded to three million customers over the span of 10 years.

In summary, the reason for Edison's success was his ability to make his invention appeal to others. He knew that people wanted a light source that was cheap, safe and convenient, so he gave them what they wanted. He also made a great effort to promote his products. In the end, people did not really care who had actually invented the light bulb as much as who had been the first person to bring them the massive benefit of the new invention. Therefore, hard work alone is not enough to make you rich if you are unable to sell yourself.

The Fates of Two Geniuses

Having talent is one thing. Turning your talent into profit is another, and it usually involves getting help from other people. You can consider two very great artists in history: Van Gogh and Picasso. They had a lot in common – they both had a very distinctive style of painting, and their works are among the most expensive paintings that have ever been sold. However, there was a great difference between them: while Picasso left a fortune after he died, van Gogh was penniless throughout his life. Why did this happen?

Again, it was about their respective networking skills. While van Gogh was a loner throughout his life, Picasso was an active member of many social circles. According to Professor Gregory Berns of Emory University: "Van Gogh's primary connection to the art world was through his brother, and this connection did not feed directly into the money that could have turned him into a living success." In contrast, Picasso's "wide-ranging social network, which included artists, writers and politicians, meant that he was never more than a few people away from anyone of importance in the world".

Therefore, the ability to affiliate to people, and get them to work for you, is one of the most important skills in your life. Most people understand that, and they make a great effort to expand their social network. They may attend events by the Junior Chamber International or the Rotary Club. It is not to say that this is not useful, but people usually find that no matter how frequently they go to such events, they usually cannot find the people to whom they want to connect. They fail to find anybody who is great enough to have a direct impact on their business or career. It makes them wonder: why do the important people always elude them?

The answer to this question is very simple: because those magical fairytale people do not exist! Potentially, everyone can be your next customer, employer or business partner. If you are able to impress them, even though they may not have a chance to help you at the moment, they will still refer you to other individuals they know who may be able to help you. On the other hand, if you fail to make yourself appear credible, then they will not consider you as their first choice – or will simply forget about you altogether.

In other words, social networking is not just about how many people you know, but also how much you can influence each of them. As pointed out in the first chapter, your persuasiveness very much depends on your ability to communicate in a convincing way. Unfortunately, most people do not have the right skills to do exactly that. It explains why so many single men and women fail to date a partner they want, despite all the money invested. It explains why so many salespeople have to resort to their friends and relatives after they fail to do business with the cold prospects. It also explains why so many office people are unable to get a promotion, which instead goes to some other colleague who entered the company at the same time as them.

Hopefully, you have already found the solution to these problems in this book. Despite a clear target market of salespeople, I believe this book can benefit people from all walks of life. It is sincerely hoped that you can get the most out of the book, and obtain a competitive edge that will lead you to success in life.

About the Author

Niall Cassidy has years of frontline experience in the banking and insurance industry. Since his job requires him to speak to different customers every day, and build trust with them as soon as possible, he has gained an invaluable insight into effective communication methods. A summary of his knowledge can be found in his book, the Art of Influencing Anyone, which is also applicable to other areas like dating, business networking, sales and marketing, etc.

www.ingramcontent.com/pod-product-compliance
Lightning Source LLC
Chambersburg PA
CBHW051342040426
42453CB00007B/368